W9-BKJ-198

Scarecrow Studies in Young Adult Literature
Series Editor: Patty Campbell

Scarecrow Studies in Young Adult Literature is intended to continue the body of critical writing established in Twayne's Young Adult Authors Series and to expand it beyond single-author studies to explorations of genres, multicultural writing, and controversial issues in young adult (YA) reading. Many of the contributing authors of the series are among the leading scholars and critics of adolescent literature, and some are YA novelists themselves.

The series is shaped by its editor, Patty Campbell, who is a renowned authority in the field, with a thirty-year background as critic, lecturer, librarian, and teacher of YA literature. Patty Campbell was the 2001 winner of the ALAN Award, given by the Assembly on Adolescent Literature of the National Council of Teachers of English for distinguished contribution to YA literature. In 1989 she was the winner of the American Library Association's Grolier Award for distinguished service to young adults and reading.

1. *What's So Scary about R. L. Stine?* by Patrick Jones, 1998.
2. *Ann Rinaldi: Historian and Storyteller*, by Jeanne M. McGlinn, 2000.
3. *Norma Fox Mazer: A Writer's World*, by Arthea J. S. Reed, 2000.
4. *Exploding the Myths: The Truth about Teens and Reading*, by Marc Aronson, 2001.
5. *The Agony and the Eggplant: Daniel Pinkwater's Heroic Struggles in the Name of YA Literature*, by Walter Hogan, 2001.
6. *Caroline Cooney: Faith and Fiction*, by Pamela Sissi Carroll, 2001.
7. *Declarations of Independence: Empowered Girls in Young Adult Literature, 1990–2001*, by Joanne Brown and Nancy St. Clair, 2002.
8. *Lost Masterworks of Young Adult Literature*, by Connie S. Zitlow, 2002.
9. *Beyond the Pale: New Essays for a New Era*, by Marc Aronson, 2003.
10. *Orson Scott Card: Writer of the Terrible Choice*, by Edith S. Tyson, 2003.

11. *Jacqueline Woodson: "The Real Thing,"* by Lois Thomas Stover, 2003.
12. *Virginia Euwer Wolff: Capturing the Music of Young Voices,* by Suzanne Elizabeth Reid, 2003.
13. *More Than a Game: Sports Literature for Young Adults,* Chris Crowe, 2004.
14. *Humor in Young Adult Literature,* by Walter Hogan, 2004.
15. *Life Is Tough: Guys, Growing Up, and Young Adult Literature,* by Rachelle Lasky Bilz, 2004.
16. *Sarah Dessen: From Burritos to Box Office,* by Wendy J. Glenn, 2005.
17. *Native American Characters and Themes in Young Adult Literature,* by Paulette F. Molin, 2005.
18. *Gay and Lesbian Literature for Young Adults,* by Michael Cart, 2005.

Sarah Dessen

From Burritos to Box Office

Wendy J. Glenn

Scarecrow Studies in Young Adult Literature, No. 16

THE SCARECROW PRESS, INC.
Lanham, Maryland • Toronto • Oxford
2005

SCARECROW PRESS, INC.

Published in the United States of America
by Scarecrow Press, Inc.
A wholly owned subsidary of
The Rowman & Littlefield Publishing Group, Inc.
4501 Forbes Boulevard, Suite 200, Lanham, Maryland 20706
www.scarecrowpress.com

9\07

PO Box 317
Oxford
OX2 9RU, UK

Copyright © 2005 by Wendy J. Glenn

British Library Cataloguing in Publication Information Available

Library of Congress Cataloging-in-Publication Data

Glenn, Wendy J., 1970–
    Sarah Dessen : from burritos to box office / Wendy J. Glenn.
        p. cm.— (Scarecrow studies in young adult literature ; no. 16)
    Includes bibliographical references and index.
    ISBN 0-8108-5325-6 (paper)
    1. Dessen, Sarah—Criticism and interpretation. 2. Young adult fiction,
American—History and criticism. 3. Teenage girls—Books and reading. 4.
Teenage girls in literature. 5. Sex role in literature. I. Title. II. Series: Scarecrow
studies in young adult literature ; 16

PS3554.E8455Z55 2005
813'.54—dc22
                                                                2004016058

∞™ The paper used in this publication meets the minimum requirements of
American National Standard for Information Sciences—Permanence of Paper
for Printed Library Materials, ANSI/NISO Z39.48-1992.

To Miranda and Shelby, my two little girls with great big hearts

Contents

	Preface	ix
	Acknowledgments	xi
	Chronology	xiii
Chapter 1	Living a Storied Life	1
Chapter 2	Visions, Practices, Products	11
Chapter 3	Change, Transformation, and *That Summer*	23
Chapter 4	Needing *Someone Like You* to Figure Out Me	43
Chapter 5	*Keeping the Moon* and Giving In to the Mystery of It All	59
Chapter 6	Escaping Submersion and Submission in the Nightmare of *Dreamland*	75
Chapter 7	The Strains and Refrains of *This Lullaby*	95
Chapter 8	Chaos, Control, and *The Truth About Forever*	111
Chapter 9	*How to Deal* and Where to Head from Here	133

Bibliography	141
Index	145
About the Author	149

~

Preface

On a visit to my local bookstore a few summers ago, I picked up *Keeping the Moon* in hopes of finding a novel that wouldn't require too much thinking. It was my vacation, after all. With a cover that featured images of dark sunglasses and a butterfly, I believed I was sure to find a low-stress, high-interest read just right for my lazy days in the chaise lounge. As I read just the first few pages, however, I soon learned I had purchased more than a simple beach book. Yes, the ocean setting was present and the writing style was relaxed, but the engaging characters, complex symbols, and elegant prose made me keep reading and go searching for more books by this new-to-me author, Sarah Dessen.

Dessen's body of fiction appeals to readers on many levels. Her writing style is complex yet readable, rich in meaning yet accessible. As an adult reader, I found myself drawn to her works for their passages of grace and good humor. I was reminded of the joys and frustrations I experienced during adolescence, those years that seemed to last an eternity at the time but now seem to have passed when I wasn't looking. With her wit and insight, Dessen takes older readers back. With her honesty and sensitivity, she moves adolescent readers forward. Dessen's novels offer not only high-quality writing but characters who experience life as young people do, featuring teens working to figure out who they are, upon whom they can depend, and how to assert their place in an increasingly complex world. Dessen speaks to her readers, taking on weighty issues with skill and intention, refusing to talk down to the young people who find themselves both lost and found in the fictional worlds she creates. She knows how to balance the heavy with the light, weaving humor and quirkiness into stories that deal with themes weighty with emotional baggage.

Each of the six young adult novels Dessen has published has received critical acclaim within the world of adolescent literature, as evidenced by successful reviews and accolades in the form of literary awards. Several key patterns emerge in the discussion and evaluation of Dessen's novels. In her fiction, she explores the complexity of human relationships between and among characters, undermines expected gender expectations, develops the themes of self-perception and identity, creates eccentric and memorable secondary characters, and uses humor to help readers bear the angst of teenage life. Because Dessen's body of fiction contains just six titles, my work explores deeply each of her novels, tracing the existence of the above-noted patterns while seeking the distinctive flavor that sets each work apart from the others.

My decision to grab that seemingly innocuous book off the shelf a few years back resulted in much more than I bargained for. Not only was I was introduced to the works of an author with a gift for crafting poignant, real stories, but I also learned that a book presumably suited for summer reading can be intricate and inspiring—and unforgettable.

~

Acknowledgments

Special thanks go to Sarah Dessen for her talent as a writer and genuineness as a person. I appreciate especially her willingness to share some time and a bit of herself during the personal interview and follow-up email exchanges. All otherwise uncredited quotes from Sarah Dessen are from the interview conducted by the author via telephone on July 3, 2003.

I am also indebted to Patty Campbell for her invitation to complete this project and the editorial guidance and good cheer she provided throughout the process. From discussions of life with a new baby to frog jumping to the search for a title, our conversations have been both fun and fruitful.

My colleagues and friends at the University of Connecticut deserve a candy bar or two on me for their ever-present support and entertaining lunchtime banter.

For their passion about YA literature and the young people who read it, Alleen Nilsen and Ken Donelson have special places in my heart.

As ever, my husband, Martin, was there all along the way.

Chronology

1970	Sarah Dessen born on June 6 in Evanston, Illinois.
1973	Moves with her parents and older brother to Chapel Hill, North Carolina.
1978	Begins writing in a quiet corner of the family room at age eight.
1988	Graduates from Chapel Hill High School. Begins college at the University of North Carolina at Greensboro as an advertising major; leaves within the year.
1989	Begins college at the University of North Carolina at Chapel Hill. Enrolls in Doris Betts' creative writing class at the University of North Carolina at Chapel Hill and is inspired to become a professional writer.
1993	Graduates with an honors degree in creative writing from the University of North Carolina at Chapel Hill; continues working as a waitress at the Flying Burrito, Chapel Hill.
1994–1996	Works as a personal assistant to Southern writer Lee Smith.
1996	Publishes *That Summer*.

1997   Accepts a position as lecturer in creative writing at the University of North Carolina at Chapel Hill. *That Summer* named an ALA Best Book for Young Adults.

1998   Publishes *Someone Like You*. *Someone Like You* named a *School Library Journal* Best Book of the Year and barnesandnoble.com Top Ten Teen Novel.

1999   Publishes *Keeping the Moon*. *Someone Like You* named an ALA Best Book for Young Adults and ALA Quick Pick for Reluctant Readers. *Keeping the Moon* named a *School Library Journal* Best Book of the Year.

2000   Publishes *Dreamland*. *Keeping the Moon* named a New York Public Library Book for the Teen Age, ALA Best Book for Young Adults, and ALA Quick Pick for Reluctant Readers. Marries Jay, her high school sweetheart, on June 10. *Dreamland* named an Amazon.com Editor's Choice.

2000–2001   *Someone Like You* named recipient of the Maryland Library Association Black-Eyed Susan Award, South Carolina Young Adult Book Award, and Missouri Gateway Readers' Choice Award for Teens.

2001   *Keeping the Moon* named an International Reading Association Young Adult Choice. *Dreamland* named an ALA Best Book for Young Adults and New York Public Library Book for the Teen Age.

2002   *Dreamland* named a New York Public Library Book for the Teen Age. Publishes *This Lullaby*. *This Lullaby* named an Original Voices Selection, Borders Group.

2002–2003   *Dreamland* named recipient of the Missouri Gateway Readers' Choice Award for Teens.

2003   *Dreamland* named an ALA Popular Paperback for Young Adults. *This Lullaby* named an ALA Best Book for Young Adults, *Los Angeles Times* Book Prize Finalist, Michigan Thumbs Up! Award Honor Book, and New York Public Library Book for the Teen Age. Film, *How to Deal* (adapted from *That Summer* and *Someone Like You*), released.

2004   Publishes *The Truth About Forever*. *This Lullaby* named a New York Public Library Book for the Teen Age.

CHAPTER ONE

~

Living a Storied Life

Sarah Dessen entered the young adult literature scene a scant eight years ago. In that time, she has written six novels for adolescents, each of which has received critical acclaim and accolades in the form of positive reviews and awards. *That Summer* (1996), *Someone Like You* (1998), *Keeping the Moon* (1999), *Dreamland* (2000), *This Lullaby* (2002), and *The Truth About Forever* (2004) comprise her current body of work and reflect the talents of an author who knows how to tell a good story.

The Earliest Influences

Dessen began her writing career at the age of eight. Tucked in the corner of her family's television room, she click-clacked away on an old typewriter her parents gave her as a gift. She created elaborate tales featuring her stuffed animals and dollhouse families as main characters. From these stories about her inanimate playmates to a Revolutionary War series inspired by a fifth-grade teacher, Dessen's craft had an early start. Her active childhood imagination has remained intact, evidenced by her current tendency to embellish, a weakness she associates with writers of fiction. "Once you learn how to make a story better," she admits, "it's hard not to do it all the time."[1]

Although born in Evanston, Illinois, in 1970, Dessen considers herself the only true Southerner in her family (and the only one with a true accent). Her mother, from New York City, and father, from Baltimore, moved to Chapel Hill, North Carolina, to accept teaching positions at the university when Dessen was three years old. Her parents, particularly her mother, have influenced strongly the person she has become and the writing that she does. Due to her parents' academic careers (her mom is a classicist, and her dad teaches Shakespeare), she grew up in a bookish home. Although she loved to read, she would occasionally get frustrated with her mother when she received books for Christmas presents instead of sweaters and jewelry, the gifts her friends were getting. In retrospect, however, Dessen admits that these works shaped her fiction. Her mother often exposed her to good books with strong female characters, a recurring element in Dessen's own novels. She has particularly powerful memories of reading the descriptive details in Lois Lowry's *A Summer to Die* and Judy Blume's *Are You There God? It's Me, Margaret*. "Back then," she claims, "books were still somewhat new to me, and when I found an author who seemed to say just what I was feeling, it really struck me and resonated. I hope that my books do that for the people who read them: I think it's the best thing to which any writer can aspire."[2]

Although she admits to times when she wanted her mother to give her the necessary space to grow, she recognizes her mother as a positive, stable force in her life. In discussing this relationship, Dessen says, "My mom and I are definitely very close, and I think that closeness always will cause some kind of issue. You're either loving each other to death or you're driving each other crazy." The mothers in Dessen's novels represent the various images she has held about her mother over the years. For example, they are sometimes overbearing, like Halley's mom in *Someone Like You*, or in need of a daughter's support, like Haven's mom in *That Summer*. Dessen describes her mother as an academic, a very smart woman, and an individual who chooses not to be like everybody else. Dessen's mother instilled in her daughter these same virtues, raising her to believe that she could achieve anything she set out to do.

Dessen remembers vividly a conversation she and her mother shared regarding Barbie dolls (a conversation that made such an impression that Dessen found a way to weave it into *Dreamland*). While Dessen was growing up, her mother, an ardent feminist, was opposed to anything Barbie. After her daughter's persistent pleas, however, she allowed her to purchase some dolls and join in the play of her neighborhood friends—on one condition. Each Barbie had to have a history—a life, a personality, a uniqueness—that set her apart from the others. Dessen's mother especially enjoyed her daughter crafting the dolls as working women. She wanted her daughter to see beyond the pretty Barbie figure and think about what she could accomplish regardless of gender, a gesture Dessen has come to value and appreciate. "The single greatest gift my mother has given me," she says, "is that I never thought there was something I couldn't do because I was a girl. There are a lot of things I can't do, like draw, and I could not be a parachute jumper because I'm scared of heights. There are a lot of reasons why I couldn't do a lot of things but never would it occur to me that because I was a girl I couldn't do them."

A Passion Lost and Found

In her later school years, Dessen describes herself as busy messing around and getting into trouble. She claims, "I wasn't a particularly memorable student, not bad, not stellar . . . I spent a lot of time in the parking lot."[3] Despite her parents' affiliation with the university, she limited her activities on campus to sneaking cigarettes behind the Morehead Planetarium. Dessen admits that she ran with a wilder crowd and wonders if she should admit this to readers. She stands by her past, however, saying, "Everything that I did in high school—good and bad—has made me the person, the writer, that I am, and for that reason I wouldn't change my experiences for anything."[4] Dessen's senior quote (from Pink Floyd) seems to say it all: "The time is gone, the song is over, thought I'd something more to say."[5] Indeed she did. Her advice to student writers reflects her own experience: "Not everybody hits their stride in high school. For most of us, in fact, it takes a little longer than just those three or four years to find yourself, so you shouldn't be discouraged if it seems like everyone else has it together. Your time is coming, and it may be closer than you think."[6]

As is the case for many adolescents, Dessen's friends were her mainstay during these exploratory years. Dessen gravitated toward girls who were more outgoing than herself, girls she has come to characterize as "the bolder, the stronger."[7] During high school, she was known as "the tall one" or "So-and-so's friend." Being the more passive participant in these relationships allowed her to develop a writer's eye and become an acute observer of human behavior. Like most of her female protagonists, Dessen watched her friends' outward actions while she tried to make sense of herself internally. In deference to friends, Dessen says, "I learned early on that your girlfriends are sometimes the only people you can really rely on when things get sticky. I always think that I get the best parts of myself from what my friends have taught me about strength and loyalty and spirit. Plus they make me laugh still and remind me where I've come from even as I'm so focused on where I'm going."[8]

As for the males in her life during this time, Dessen did not find herself attracted to the often-touted boy with the broad football shoulders or chiseled soccer calves. Instead, she was interested in the guy who was different and funny and weird, the guy who was not so caught up in appearances and was willing to say, "You don't have to be perfect. I like it better that you're not."[9] Sumner, the primary male character in *That Summer*, serves as the first incarnation of this boy in her writing. With his quirky mannerisms and penchant for foolishness and play, he represents the free-spirited young man most likely to sweep Dessen off her feet (and be celebrated in her novels).

Although much of Dessen's material is drawn from her high school days, she wrote only reluctantly during most of this time, primarily due to frustration over the fact that writing in her later school years was prescriptive and academic, that "there were always rules about what you were Supposed to Write."[10] She remembers having the opportunity to write creatively in elementary and middle school, but, in high school, making up her own tales was not valued in the English classroom. She was frustrated by the fact that "all writing had to be so structured, everything outlined carefully" and wished instead that her teachers had let students explore their creative side, to "take a leap and really stretch in their own writing."[11] She hoped for more when she enrolled in a writers' workshop class during her junior year, but perception did not fit reality. Although she found herself encouraged to write about topics of her choosing, she was still forced to include a minimum number of adverb phrases and participle clauses.

Dessen found limited pleasure in writing during her senior year but not enough to inspire her to consider herself a writer. When the one creative writing teacher in the school left after Dessen's junior year, students that were enrolled in his courses were farmed into other classes. Dessen and eleven other young writers ended up in a class with a teacher who had never taught creative writing. He told his students to write about whatever they wanted. Dessen remembers this as being both incredibly liberating and terrifying at the same time. She could finally write as she desired, but, without any guidance, the writing remained dark and depressing, caught up in the angst of adolescence.

After high school, Dessen attended the University of North Carolina at Greenboro as an advertising major. Shortly thereafter, she dropped out and returned to Chapel Hill, realizing that life in the corporate world was not for her. Upon her return, her mother encouraged her to enroll in a creative writing class taught by Doris Betts, a Southern writer teaching at the University of North Carolina at Chapel Hill. Dessen sat next to Betts on the first day, looked at her, and realized that she, too, wanted to become a writer. The class reconnected her with writing, and in 1993, after five years at Chapel Hill, Dessen graduated with highest honors from the English Department's creative writing program.

A Risky Venture

Despite her success at the university, Dessen had a hard time envisioning herself as a working writer. Fortunately, she was able to witness this reality in her hometown. Chapel Hill is home to many writers and a flourishing North Carolina writing group. As a result, Dessen saw many authors whose works she had read flitting out and about town. They were real people living real lives. "At that age," she remembers, "you're so used to reading books and the people who have written them are either dead or you'd never imagine that they could actually be at the store buying lettuce." Dessen learned from these models and mentors that it was possible for her to be a real, money-earning writer.

So, instead of drafting a resume and donning a pair of pantyhose, Dessen continued waiting tables at the Flying Burrito Restaurant while beginning a writing routine at night and living in what she describes as a "ramshackle little house."[12] She sometimes questioned her choice, especially when she compared herself with her college friends who had company cars and real salaries. Dessen's parents provided the necessary support, paying for her healthcare and believing in her talent. When she came home after being on the five and a half year plan in college and said, "Well, I think I'm not going to get a real job. I'm going to go wait tables and try to publish a novel instead," she would not have blamed them if they had responded, "No, put on a suit. Go get a job." But they encouraged her to see her passion through, perhaps due to their academic training. They appreciated that writing could be a job, one in which their daughter could excel. Although she had written only one rather unimpressive novel during her senior year of college and begun just one other, Dessen accepted their support and took the risk. In retrospect, she says, "At times it seemed really stupid, since I was totally broke and there was no kind of guarantee that I'd ever see anything come of it. Luckily, it did. But even if I hadn't sold a book by now I'd still be writing. It becomes a part of you, just something you do."[13]

As luck would have it, Dessen took a class from famed Southern writer Lee Smith, who ultimately set her up with her first book contract. Smith hired her as a part-time personal assistant, a job that saw Dessen spending ample time walking the dog and running to the post office. As a reward for these tasks, Smith willingly read Dessen's drafts. Upon reading one novel that she believed had particular promise, Smith sent the manuscript to her own agent. Although the agent enjoyed the story, she was not able to sell it. Smith mentioned that Dessen had written another novel, one with a young protagonist, that might appeal to young adult readers. Shortly thereafter, and three years after graduating, Dessen sold her first book. She received the call from her agent as she was leaving to meet a friend at a local bagel shop. She grabbed her friend and headed to her parents' house where she could use their fax machine to access the offer letter. As she, her friend, and her dad munched on bagels, details regarding the contract were discussed and decided. Dessen had to return to work at the restaurant that night but remembers how odd it felt to be serving burritos to patrons as a now published author.

At this point, little changed in her life. *That Summer* came out in October, but she continued to wait tables by day and write at night. Just less than a year later, however, Dessen turned in her apron and notepad for a job as a creative writing lecturer at the University of North Carolina at Chapel Hill. Marianne Gingher, director of Carolina's creative writing program, heard Dessen read excerpts from *That Summer* at the Bull's Head Bookshop and offered her a job on the spot. Dessen misses, on occasion, life as a waitress, noting, "It was a great job for a writer. Endless conversations to eavesdrop, tons of material, and fast money without ever taking work home. Plus, free Mexican food, the best perk of all."[14]

Dessen never intended to be a YA writer. She simply wrote a book that featured a fifteen-year-old narrator with a strong voice. Even now, with six young adult novels under her belt, Dessen rarely reads other YA authors, claiming she would worry about how her work compares to theirs. Instead, she writes the kinds of books that she likes to read. She is intrigued, especially, by the potential that exists during the adolescent years when young people are "on the verge of a big change."[15] She admits that her own teen years were "plagued with this awful uncertainty" and insecurity about who she was and her place in the world.[16] Dessen hopes the message she is sending to young readers is to believe in themselves even when they feel incredibly alone. It is obvious that she is comfortable in the teenage voice. She writes, "Even though it was in a way accidental, I've found that writing for teens suits me. I do short stories, and other novels, that are for an older audience, but again and again I am brought back to the stories of high school. Maybe it's because so much happened to me then that I'm not finished yet telling everything."[17] For that, we, as readers, are grateful.

A Worthwhile Investment

Currently, Dessen teaches "Introduction to Fiction Writing" and "Intermediate Fiction Writing" at UNC–Chapel Hill in the same program where she did her own undergraduate work. Her youth sometimes poses a problem. The first time she entered the faculty mailroom, an administrative assistant attempted to chase her out, thinking she was a student. She loves her work as a writing teacher, however, claiming, "I get to show people how writing can really change the way you see not only yourself but the world. I've found in my own life that if my writing isn't going well, not much else will. It is the one constant, the key to everything else."[18]

Living in the same town where she grew up and experienced the time of life she describes in her books, Dessen relishes the opportunity to relive her teen days. She explains, "It's a lot easier to write about high school when you're in the same place you were when you were in high school. If I was living in New York City and in an apartment, it would be hard for me to remember what it was like driving home on a summer evening with my friends through the fields around here. But now I do it, so it's very easy for me to be like, oh, this is like a Saturday night when I was fifteen."

Dessen lives in the country with her husband (her high school boyfriend), some lizards, and two dogs that she loves to spoil. She enjoys gardening and shopping, admitting an addiction to the Gap clearance rack and the black pants she strives to find hanging there. She has a penchant for Starbucks mochas, *People* magazine, and Oprah, and makes a delectable bean salad. A celebrity and pop culture junkie, she was thrilled to see her name in *Entertainment Weekly* upon the release of the film, *How to Deal*, based on her first two novels, *That Summer* and *Someone Like You*. She likes to think, however, that her books are much more exciting than she is, and that that is a good thing. She believes that "it's always more fun to make stuff up anyway."[19]

Notes

1. Sarah Dessen, "Biography," *Personal Website*, at www.sarahdessen.com/bio.html (accessed 28 February 2003).

2. Dessen, "Biography," *Personal Website*.

3. "An Interview with Sarah Dessen," *Razorbill*, at www.razorbillzine.com/interviewsd.html (accessed 4 March 2003).

4. Don Gallo, "Interview with Sarah Dessen," *authors4teens*, at www.authors4teens.com/index.asp (accessed 2 April 2004).

5. Dessen, "Biography," *Personal Website*.

6. "An Interview with Sarah Dessen," *Razorbill*.

7. "An Interview with Sarah Dessen," *DreamGirl Magazine*, at www.dgarts.com/content/saradessen.htm (accesssed 4 March 2003).

8. "An Interview with Sarah Dessen," *DreamGirl Magazine*.

9. "An Interview with Sarah Dessen," *BWI*, at http://www.bwibooks.com/sdessen.htm (accessed 2 April 2004).

10. Sarah Dessen, "Frequently Asked Questions," *Personal Website*, at www.sarahdessen.com/faq.html (accessed 28 February 2003).

11. Gallo, "Interview with Sarah Dessen," *authors4teens*.
12. Dessen, "Biography," *Personal Website*.
13. Dessen, "Frequently Asked Questions," *Personal Website*.
14. Dessen, "Biography," *Personal Website*.
15. "An Interview with Sarah Dessen," *BWI*.
16. Gallo, "Interview with Sarah Dessen," *authors4teens*.
17. Dessen, "Biography," *Personal Website*.
18. Dessen, "Biography," *Personal Website*.
19. Dessen, "Biography," *Personal Website*.

~

...ns, Practices, Products

When speaking of herself as an author, Dessen provides a glimpse into her writer's mind, thus allowing us to read her works with a unique perspective that she alone can share. We can explore the extent to which her writing beliefs and behaviors are reflected in the novels she composes and examine the relationship between a writer's thoughts and a writer's craft.

The Confidence to Commit

Dessen admits that writing is not always painless. In both earnest and jest, she says, "I don't like it when writers act like writing is easy. Maybe it is for them. In which case, I hate them. I just don't trust writers who say, oh, it's great. I don't think anyone's that confident about what they're writing." Although she is disciplined and writes every day while working on a novel, Dessen does not leap to her desk each afternoon, filled with ideas and enthusiasm, raring to go. She usually has to drag herself to the computer and fight the urge to turn on *Oprah* or go shopping instead. Yet, she refuses to behave like those people who spend time talking about the novel they have always wanted to write rather than just writing it. She advises young writers, "If you want to be a writer, it should be a main and basic part of your daily life. Take it seriously and do the work."[1]

It is not always easy, however, to muster the confidence needed to face the blinking cursor each day, especially when the words just don't seem to flow. Although people may assume that having successfully written a novel means doing it with ease again in the future, Dessen knows from experience that there are no guarantees when it comes to the creative process. She believes that writing differs from other professions, in that, "If you have a job where you do the same thing every day, you don't doubt yourself. If you're a typist, you don't go to work and think, What if I can't type today? You can. If you're a carpenter, you don't go to work and think, What if I can't hammer this nail today? Because you know you can; you did it yesterday." When asked why she writes despite these stresses, Dessen notes in her characteristically humble and humorous way, "It is one of the only things I'm good at. I'm very subpar in just about everything else."

A self-professed organizer, Dessen believes that fate made her a writer simply to remind her that she has less control over things than she would like to believe. She regrets the time she has spent fighting a scene that isn't progressing as she desires and works daily at learning to "step back, take a deep breath, and trust the story."[2] It is the unknowns associated with writing that both frustrate and excite her. She is driven by those rare moments when things are just clicking, those once-every-three-days days when everything shifts and comes together. She loves the excitement that is generated when she is thinking about a new book that she has not yet started—all the potential and possibility. While this potential and possibility are being explored in her mind and on the page, she also relishes letting her characters play out their lives in her head alone. She refuses to share her novels with anyone until they are done and she is content with them, saying, "Writing a novel is like keeping the best secret ever: the minute you tell anyone, it lessens it a bit. So I like to hold it all in as long as possible."[3] Until the work is progress is finally published, even her husband is left to wonder why Dessen asks him random questions like, "What's the name of a kind of fishing lure? Or, How many songs can you think of that have to do with cars?"[4]

Dessen defines writing as a personal act, one that reflects her vision and one in which she takes great pride. As a result, when writing, she doesn't approach her books wondering what others might think. In writing the initial draft, in particular, she writes for herself and no one else. Although the opinions of her editors enter into the revision process, Dessen refuses to relinquish control over an element in a story that she believes is essential. This does not mean, however, that the opinions of others do not matter to her. Two reviews of her books have been less than positive; one, in particular, was for her second book, *Someone Like You*, in the *Daily Tar Heel*, the Chapel Hill university newspaper. Although the same book received a positive review in the *New York Times Book Review* that same week, Dessen carried the negative review in her purse for over a year. Perfectionist that she is, she obsessed over every scathing detail, rereading the review and sharing it with others to no end. When thinking about the negative commentary directed toward her works, she reports, "It stings, you feel worthless and pathetic, you move on. I make a point of sitting down and writing after every bad review, just to remind myself that it can't have anything to do with my work."[5] Yet, it wasn't until her best friend flushed the rotten review at a wedding that the critic's words finally left her side.

The Writer's Vision

Dessen refuses to represent her works as something they are not. She believes that she simply writes books that she hopes will resonate with readers. Her primary goal is to create works that remain relevant several years after they are released and continue to attract new readers who enjoy the story. As a member of the academic community, the incongruity between her work and that of her peers rears its head every once in a while. When her fifth novel, *This Lullaby*, was nominated for a *Los Angeles Times* Book Award, Dessen received a congratulatory email from a university administrator who noted how much he appreciated her scholarship. Dessen just laughed. She admits, "Never in my life would I have thought of my books as scholarship. The main thing is not to let it get too into something it's not. I just really love writing." Dessen describes most of the professors with whom she teaches creative writing as serious poets. She considers herself a serious author but doesn't take her books more seriously than they need to be taken. "I don't think that I am writing *Absolom, Absolom*. I know that I'm not," she says. "But I am reaching the exact kind of reader that I am, the kind of reader who just wants a good story and some fun characters that they can relate to."

Dessen didn't always possess this confident vision of herself as a writer. She went through a period in college during which she attempted to write like everyone else in her writing workshop. She created dark, depressing stories that were bloated with meaning but felt that they did not reflect her real self. Her closest friends, who had been reading her works since she was in high school, told her the truth, saying, "This is terrible. This isn't you."[6] With time and increasing confidence in herself and her skill, Dessen realized that the stories she was writing about girls, friends, family, and growing up reflected her best—and most honest—writing.

Not having set out to write with the teen reader in mind, Dessen admits that her knowledge of these readers is still in the process of development. She finds it easier to picture them now, however, because she hears from them regularly, something she finds both rewarding and unexpected. With this newfound awareness of who these young readers are and what they value, Dessen possesses an increasingly clear vision of the readers for whom she is writing. Her books are girl-centered with the protagonists serving as the embodiment of the kind of girl she imagines selecting one of her books off of the shelf. They are girls who tend to be less dynamic, hanging back and reporting on events while a more aggressive friend lives a louder life. These observers tend to learn about themselves as a result of their outsider status, however. At the start, they may wish that they could be more like their more gregarious peers but come to learn that even the girls who seem most confident often don't see themselves in that way. For each of her heroines, Dessen "provides a credible voice and even more credible viewpoint; as these girls untangle emotions and situations for which schools and parents have failed to prepare them, they remain absolutely authentic in their reactions and behavior."[7] Dessen has a harder time imagining young males reading her novels. Dessen claims that because she was never a teenage boy, she is not able to capture the male experience in the same way she can as a female writer writing for females.

Although Dessen's books enjoy a strong following among adolescent girls, Dessen likes to think that her books are not just for teens.

The issues adolescents face do not magically disappear as we are handed our diploma and walk off the stage as high school graduates. When explaining why her family and friends, adults well beyond their adolescent years, enjoy her novels, she says, "The same issues will continue to come up throughout your life, maybe in different incarnations. It's one thing that we all have in common. We were all that age."

A self-professed romantic, Dessen loves a happy ending and strives to leave readers feeling good. She thrives on her capacity to imagine. Always dreaming in her own head, she looks around and not only notices the world as it is, but asks how it might be different. Although YA literature has the reputation of often being dark and heavy, Dessen's works address serious issues while remaining basically optimistic in tone. As a reader, Dessen is disappointed when she invests her time in a book and is left with a depressing ending. In most of her novels, the second to last chapter serves the purpose of wrapping up the plot. The final chapter, however, serves as "icing on the cake," involving a final scene of great humor or sweetness. Dessen's editors repeatedly attempt to cut that last chapter, but Dessen fights for her artistic vision, arguing, "We all want happy endings. Who doesn't want a happy ending? I don't want to hang out with people like that."

The Process

Dessen follows a writing routine. Before she begins any new novel, she has already envisioned the first chapter, last chapter, and climax. Although these benchmarks are not set in stone, they serve as a guide to ensure that the work stays on track. Dessen has started books and found herself three hundred pages in with nothing of note having happened. She argues that, when it comes to writing, some planning is essential. She offers the following comparison:

> It's like going on a trip. Very rarely do you just pack a bag, get in the car, and start driving. Even if you don't want to be tied down to a total itinerary, you have a general sense. OK, I'm going to go to DC, but maybe if I see something interesting along the way, I'll pull off. Maybe I'll stop here and sleep on these peoples' couch. It's just generally having a sense

of, a skeleton of the story, so there's something to follow, something that you are working up toward.

Dessen is particularly invested in her first line. She patiently awaits its inspired arrival, and, once it makes an appearance, diligent, daily writing begins.

In gathering information for her novels, Dessen conducts informal research. In preparation for *Someone Like You*, she visited her local library to determine whether or not the dates for Halley's comet would allow for her protagonist to have seen it as a young girl. To ensure a plausible description of the pregnancy of a secondary character in the novel, she referred to the popular text *What to Expect When You're Expecting* [8] and developed a timeline delineating what the character would experience when. Her understanding of the abusive relationship in *Dreamland* was more a result of acquired knowledge than personal experience or formal research. While in college, Dessen enrolled in several psychology classes and studied the battered women syndrome. Reading several articles in popular women's magazines also gave her insight into the warning signs associated with abusive relationships, many of which emerge in the development of Caitlin's character over the course of the novel. Although she writes for teens, Dessen does not work to stay abreast of current trends for the sake of her readers. She does it to feed her own pop culture addiction instead. She admits, "I would love to say that I subscribe to all the magazines that I subscribe to because of that because it sounds to scholarly, but it's not true. I love *US Weekly*. I love *People Magazine*. I watch MTV because I like MTV." Most of Dessen's research, however, comes from life itself. She remains aware of the world, keeping her eyes open for the stories that surround her in her daily interactions and observations.

The Teaching–Writing Connection

Dessen's teaching informs her writing and vice versa. Having to face a classroom of would-be writers each day forces her to practice what she preaches. She must demonstrate the discipline and hard work that she claims goes into successful writing. Working with students has made her realize just how hard she is on herself. She expects much of her students (and herself) and considers herself a critical reader who demands a serious commitment to the craft. Dessen also enjoys the opportunity to interact with her students, to break free from the solitary life that writing entails. Her students expose her to new opinions, new views on the world of stories and the world at large. They also serve as literary critics. When each new books comes out, Dessen says her students will "all come out when I read. They'll all sit in the back and giggle, and then they'll bring my book to me and show me sentences that they think I should have done better."[9]

When asked whether or not writing can be taught, Dessen offers a balanced response. Among the twenty or so students she has in a given class, Dessen assumes a few will have some innate talent for writing. They possess a comfort with the craft, an ear for language and speech that cannot be learned in a writing classroom. She likens writing to painting, noting, "Just as there are people in art classes who can come in and immediately do a beautiful painting while the rest of us are dabbing on our easel, there are students who enter the classroom with the ability to write well."

Conversely, there are students who, at the start, have little understanding of writing as a craft. With time and good instruction, they may, by the end, have a good sense of story—a clearer knowledge of plot and character development, for example. With these struggling students, sometimes the problem is simply a result of what they are choosing to write about. They attempt to write stories about things that aren't dear to them. As soon as they take a risk and write about something that is close to their hearts, all of their writing opens up. With these students, Dessen is also fighting against what they have been taught in high school. She repeatedly assures students that they can use contractions when writing dialogue, for example. She is careful, however, not to condemn classroom teachers, explaining, "I'm not trying to disparage the teachers whose job it is and whose jobs are often on the line. I don't think that going through the school system necessarily results in turning you into a writer. They're teaching you how to write a paper. They're teaching you how to write in expository style. But they're not really teaching you about the art of writing."

The Inspiration of Life on Literature

Life and literature overlap to some extent in Dessen's works. All good fiction, she professes, begins with some truth. In developing her stories, then, she begins with her own experiences or those of people close to her. This is easier given the fact that Dessen remains a resident in the town in which she lived during her high school years. She continues to be close with friends from that time and occasionally bumps into homeroom companions and former crushes while pumping gas or buying stamps. It is easy, then, to put herself back into that place, that voice.

The inspiration for several of her novels can be traced to particular events in her life. The weddings in *That Summer* parallel her cousin's wedding, an event that was emotional for Dessen in that it forced her to start thinking about the responsibilities that come with adulthood. Like Haven, the female protagonist, Dessen also enjoyed a short stint as a sales clerk in a mall shoe store and was fired during the big Hot Diggety Days Sales Event. *Someone Like You* was based, in part, on the death of the most popular boy in her ninth-grade class who was killed in a motorcycle accident. This resulted in her first experience with the death of someone her age and associated feelings of confusion and imbalance. *Keeping the Moon* was inspired by her work as a waitress and reflects the self-confidence she developed as a result of this career endeavor. Colie's character was inspired by kids who were picked on in school as featured on a daytime talk show. With respect to *Dreamland*, Dessen was never in an abusive relationship like that of Caitlin. She believes that there is some root of the story buried down deep that is related to her in some way, especially when she reflects on a dark period during her senior year when she experienced depression and wanted to lose herself in something, anything, rather than face her problems. *The Truth About Forever* emerged out of Dessen's reflection on questions related to the chaos in the world occurring just before she began the book—"Why do bad things happen? Why can't we stop them? What can we do to make the world safer?"[10] The illness and death of a neighbor Dessen's age and her resulting feelings of helplessness compounded her sense of uncertainty in the world. It is difficult to distance Dessen's life from her writing, as writing is, in many ways, her life.

Dessen is quick to note, however, that fiction is often more engaging and interesting than real life. Although she may begin with a familiar experience, she veers off into the world of fiction rather quickly:

> The trick is to begin with what really happened, and then change it to what you wish had happened, or what you wish you'd said. Sometimes the truth just reads flatter than fiction: a lot of times I'll tell my students I don't think a particular story seems plausible, and they'll argue, "But it did happen! Just like that!" The thing is that it may have happened, but maybe they're so close to it they're not filling in the full picture. Too much truth makes you assume things, whereas in true fiction you have to paint the entire picture.[11]

Themes in Dessen's Works

Defining Relationships

Dessen understands relationships in their many forms. Whether focusing on familial, peer, or romantic entanglements, she recognizes the dynamic nature of these relationships as well as the fact that some are healthier than others. In her novels, we see how our lives are shaped by the relationships we form and break. These help to determine who we are and what we become. Positive relationships remain true even when we feel weak, making us stronger than we could ever be alone. Negative relationships trap us and deny us opportunities to grow. Dessen encourages us to surround ourselves with good people.

In her novels, Dessen pays particular attention to gendered relationships, exploring the varying roles that women and men play in one another's lives. The feminist underpinnings that shape Dessen's work likely sprout from her affinity for writings by and about strong Southern women. She cites Fannie Flagg's *Coming Attractions* as a novel that inspired her to become a writer due, in part, to the feisty female voice that it contains. Dessen's women, although not always in agreement, share a common bond that unites them even in the hardest of times. This shared existence by virtue of a shared "femaleness" creates a sense of community among Dessen's women. Even when a mother fails to live up to her daughter's expectations, for example, mother and daughter recognize the value of the relationship they share. Every significant flawed female character in Dessen's novels is eventually redeemed.

The males, however, do not all enjoy this shot at redemption. The men and boys who inhabit Dessen's novels tend to fall into one of three categories—the absent, the deceptive, and the sweet. From the father who abandons his child (*This Lullaby*) to the stepfather who cheats on his new wife (*This Lullaby*) to the boyfriend who hits (*Dreamland*) to the young artist who heals (*Keeping the Moon*), we are given a glimpse of a full range of male behavior. In her novels, Dessen condemns those men who fit traditional, patriarchal norms and celebrates those who nurture and care. The most worthy men in her novels are either quirky and funny or more serious and quiet, providing a parallel to the relationships she has with the two most important men in her life, her comedic husband and academic father. When it comes to the development of her admirable male characters, she worries about repeating herself. Although she doesn't want to have too many guys fall into the same "good guy" category, she believes strongly that there is something to be said for that kind of guy, the sensitive, sweet, and mildly eccentric young man who doesn't spend his days swapping stories with his buddies in the locker room. Although Dessen believes that people assume girls want the hunky male athlete, she says, "We're not all going to get that boy. Nor do we all want that boy. Believe me, we don't want that boy."

Seeking Personal Identity

Dessen encourages the acceptance of self in her writings, noting that what we believe about ourselves weighs more heavily than external reality or the views of others. When we are confident and trusting in who we are, this power of perception allows us to be strong even when others see us as weak. When we see ourselves as less than we are, however, we allow a faulty perception to determine our reality, and even the most flattering of compliments will not alter our vision of self unless we are willing to make this change. It is only when we look within to determine who we really are, to match perception and reality, that we find the freedom to become what we will. Dessen says that her books are about girls "on the verge of a big change. They're aware that their world is changing, but they're not aware that they're going to have to change with it."

For Dessen, the process of finding one's self has followed her into her adult life. She recognizes a clear connection between her work as a writer and her growth as a person. Even if she doesn't see it during the time that she is working on a novel, her own struggles with personal identity surface in the text on the page. She remembers writing *This Lullaby* and feeling insecure due to frustration over having just written a not-very-good book. Committing to *This Lullaby* required a leap of faith that was ultimately embodied in the final product. It is seen in the character of Remy who must accept that you cannot control everything and must, at times, just jump in and hope for the best. And it is evident in the parallel plot line that sees Remy's mother writing her own novel in the duration of the story. Dessen recognizes the connection as well, noting, "When Remy's mom was freaking out, that's when I was freaking out. For Remy to be saying to her mom, 'You always do this. You do this every book. You'll be fine.' It's Remy talking to me."

Creating a Community

While reading one of Dessen's novels, one can't help but feel a part of the community. Dessen has an incredible ability to create a network of characters who weave their way in and out of the female protagonist's life. Each young speaker is surrounded by a cast of characters that breathes a sense of reality into the world she inhabits. As we peer into this community, we come to know intimately the people who share and shape her daily life. Her characters do not act in isolation. As in our lives, each influences and is influenced by those who share his or her geographical space. Perhaps this sense of community is so powerfully developed because Dessen herself remains tightly linked to the community where she spent her adolescent years.

For Dessen, secondary characters serve several purposes. They pull the attention off the main character just enough so that readers can regroup. They enter at the crucial moment and say all the things that are really important. They provide comic relief. But, perhaps most significantly, they are fun to create and read about. As Dessen describes, "You can have so much fun with secondary characters. With the narrator, you have to be responsible for what they are saying. They are the center. You can be a little bit crazier with the people that are off on the side." This craziness has resulted in several unique, lovable, and memorable characters.

Allowing for Laughter

Each of Dessen's novels contains passages of laugh-aloud fun. Dessen doesn't think that she is funny necessarily but admits that she can use humor effectively. When she was in college, she often felt like she wasn't a real writer because she wrote things that were funny. She attended very serious writing workshop classes where everyone's work was mired in darkness and despair, while she composed stories about the prom that other students thought were very cute. Dessen is upset with herself that she ever doubted that what she did counted. To combat this perception, Dessen works with her students to point out that it is difficult to write humor and that many people are unable to do it. The mark of this truly gifted author resides in her ability not to just do it, but to harness humor in the most unexpected, perhaps darkest, realms of where we live, thus giving readers a chance to rise up and gasp for some air. Dessen loves writing funny scenes and wonders if it is appropriate for her to be sitting at her computer cackling away to herself over the vision she is bringing to life.

Notes

1. "An Interview with Sarah Dessen," *DreamGirl Magazine*, at www.dgarts .com/content/saradessen.htm (accesssed 4 March 2003).

2. Don Gallo, "Interview with Sarah Dessen," *authors4teens*, at www .authors4teens.com/index.asp (accessed 2 April 2004).

3. "An Interview with Sarah Dessen," *Razorbill*, at www.razorbillzine.com/ interviewsd.html (accessed 4 March 2003).

4. Gallo, "Interview with Sarah Dessen," *authors4teens*.

5. "An Interview with Sarah Dessen," *Razorbill*.

6. "An Interview with Sarah Dessen," *BWI*, at http://www.bwibooks.com/ sdessen.htm (accessed 2 April 2004).

7. Debra Mitts Smith, "Rising Star: Sarah Dessen," *The Bulletin of the Center for Children's Books*, at www.lis.uiuc.edu/puboff/bccb/0303focus.html (accessed 2 April 2004).

8. Heidi E. Murkoff, Arlene Eisenberg, and Sandee Hathaway, *What to Expect When You're Expecting* (New York: Workman Publishing, 1984).

9. "An Interview with Sarah Dessen," *BWI*.

10. "An Interview with Sarah Dessen," *BWI*.

11. "An Interview with Sarah Dessen," *DreamGirl Magazine*.

CHAPTER THREE

~

Change, Transformation, and *That Summer*

"Everyone can reach back to one summer and lay a finger to it, finding the exact point when everything changed. That summer was mine" (1). Love and loss, permanence and change, reality and fantasy. Dessen's first novel, *That Summer* (1996), embraces contradictions and demonstrates that the line between these seeming opposites can be bent, difficult to discern, even erased. Inspired by Dannye Romine Powell's poem "At Every Wedding Someone Stays Home," the novel examines relationships that exist on several levels and the changes that accompany life regardless of our willingness to accept them, all while helping us laugh at our human flaws and foibles. The work has been well-received by critics, earning the title of ALA Best Book for Young Adults, *Booklist* Best of 1996, New York Library Best Book for the Teen Age, as well as starred reviews in *Publishers Weekly*, *Booklist*, and *Kirkus Reviews*. Called an "unusually perceptive debut"[1] that is "written with such grace that you want to quote sentence after sentence,"[2] the novel is powerful in both content and form.

Dessen never set out to write a book for young adults. The novel just happens to be a book with a teenage narrator. It is the voice of this young protagonist, however, that makes the book most accessible to and engaging for teen readers, especially girls. Female readers will identify with "how it feels when your childhood friend is suddenly boy crazy, and you can't understand the language; how it hurts to break the 'tether' with your mother and to be disappointed by a charming boy."[3] They will respect the narrator's voice. Although she "recounts external events with a journalist's objective matter-of-factness,"[4] she also recognizes her blindness when it comes to making sense of her own life.

Haven, the uncomfortably tall, fifteen-year-old protagonist, begins and ends her summer with a dreaded wedding. The first involves her sportscaster father and the weather girl with whom he has had an affair. The second sees Haven's sister, Ashley, marrying Lewis, a boring, drab fellow who Haven believes has tamed her once wild and carefree sister. Between weddings, Haven spends her days working at Little Feet, a children's shoe store in the local mall, and trying to make sense of Casey, her best friend who has returned from summer camp an altered person with a new boyfriend. Feeling as though too much of her life is out of her control—a lost father, a lost sister, a lost friend—Haven finds solace in the reappearance of Sumner, one of Ashley's former boyfriends, who has the ability to make the ordinary seem extraordinary. Haven reminisces about the summer beach vacation that she, her family, and Sumner all enjoyed, back when her life seemed perfect. Her romanticized vision is fractured, however, when she learns the truth about Sumner. Haven must learn to accept the present as real, even though it is not ideal.

The Acceptance of Change

Perhaps the most powerful message contained in *That Summer* is that we lead ever-changing lives and must accept this change as a part of our growth. Although change is fearful, it is inevitable. As Heracleitus stated, we can never dip our foot into the same river twice. Circumstances, events, decisions, and a lack thereof change us whether or not we want them to. But, although the past shapes us, it cannot (and should not) hold us. The summer setting provides the ideal backdrop for the exploration of this theme. With its slow-paced, carefree cadence of days, summer affords us time to reflect, even if the results of our ponderings are difficult to accept.

These are lessons Haven must learn as her world ever shifts. She is surrounded by change. Her father's wedding signals the end of her old family. She will never again witness her father slip an arm around her mother's waist and hold her close. Her sister's upcoming wedding heightens this sense of loss. Soon her sister will become Mrs. Ashley Warsher. She will go, and Haven and her mother will be left to figure out their own relationship. Haven's dear friend, Casey, introduces a further element of change into her life when she returns home from camp where she had spent the summer flirting with boys and writing Haven long letters sealed with lipstick kisses, a far cry from the girl she once was—the small, shy, redhead who took tap-dancing lessons with her mother.

The most difficult part of dealing with these changes is that Haven feels they are occurring beyond her control; her world is being altered without her input or approval. To shield herself, she latches onto the sudden and surprising arrival of Sumner, Ashley's former boyfriend and "a symbol for Haven of that long-ago summer" before weddings, divorces, and change.[5] He is the boy with the magical personality who makes Ashley laugh, draws people out of their separate rooms, and transforms a cheap Frisbee into a symbol of a happier time. When he comes back into her life, Haven believes it is a sign. Perhaps he was meant to return to fix the craziness of her life. He serves as proof that the happier times she remembers truly did exist.

This vision of Sumner and his potential for magic give Haven hope and the belief that she has an ally despite the fact that those around her do not seem to recognize her frustrations. Sumner understands. He, too, went through the divorce of his parents. He, too, lost Ashley. When he picks Haven up in the mall security golf cart and together they fly down the corridor dodging shoppers and whirring past stores that once seemed mundane, Haven feels a sense of "hope that maybe somewhere in all this madness and confusion, he was the one who could understand [her]" (109).

When it is most needed, however, Sumner fails to give Haven what she thinks she needs. He doesn't sympathize with her plight. She confesses her exasperation over the changes in her life, blaming Ashley for setting them in motion when she sent Sumner away. Once Sumner exited their lives, everything seemed to fall apart; with him gone, the magic is gone. Haven wants Sumner to be angry right along with her, but he remains quiet, failing to admit that the break-up with Ashley was due to his own infidelity. Even without this knowledge, Haven realizes that Sumner is not the boy she envisioned. By refusing to validate her emotions, he fails her. She runs from him, realizing that he is not what she wanted him to be and perhaps never was. When Haven asks Ashley about the break-up and learns the truth about Sumner, she accepts her vision of him and the past as just that, a picture to be kept as memory. She knows that she will never see him, or the summer they shared, in the same way. He is the first boy to disappoint her; he destroys the myth she so wants to be true.

With the myth shattered, Haven is forced to accept the reality of her life, changes and all. She cannot turn back time, reunite her parents, keep Ashley home, or keep from growing up herself. She must "face forward rather than back" and "shake off her dependence on a memory of idyllic happiness."[6] She begins this process on the evening before Ashley's wedding when she, her mother, and the bride-to-be share wine and memories at the dining room table, telling the stories of the past that had been avoided and neglected since the divorce. Haven is moving on. This night provides a starting point upon which to build her future memories.

Defining One's Self-Concept

Haven's growth, both literal and figurative, is contained within her changing physical self-concept over the course of the novel. At the outset, Haven experiences discomfort due to her five-foot-eleven-inch stature. When looking in the mirror, she describes a girl composed of "lines intersecting, planes going on forever and ever, sharp to anyone who might brush against [her]" (97). As a result of this perception, Haven tries to make herself smaller, has nightmares of growing into a giant, and misses being "no bigger than a minute" as an elementary teacher once described her. At her father's wedding, she imagines that she looks like a tall, pink straw in her bridesmaid dress and feels like a man walking on stilts when she heads down the aisle. Haven has made such a habit of hiding her height and attempting to diminish her physical presence that her mother and Ashley have devised a signal, a sharp poke in the lower back, to let Haven know when she is slouching. Haven seems to carry the weight of the world on her shoulders. Her anxiety over the changes that are happening around her, her desire to support her mother and make things right again with her family, and her sadness over past and future losses weigh upon her, symbolically embodied in the physical self she puts forth. Her situation only worsens due to her unwillingness to allow others to see the pain she is experiencing and lessen her load by trusting in those who love her.

Two events lead to a significant change in Haven's self-image and subsequent physical presence. One afternoon during a "sidewalk sale" at the shoe store, she loses her cool. An overbearing customer pushes Haven too far, and Haven retaliates. She flees the mall feeling strong, supercharged with adrenaline from the conflict. Shortly thereafter, Haven challenges her father and refuses to come to his car as he waits to pick her up for their weekly father-daughter outing. In each instance, Haven asserts herself, moving from passive victim to active agent of change. She demonstrates to herself that she does not have to be a pawn in the lives of others. She can have a say in how her life turns out. Later in the day, Haven witnesses a change in her physical form when she emerges from the shower and sees herself in the mirror:

> It was as if I had grown again as I slept, but this time just to fit my own size. As if my soul had expanded, filling out the gaps of the height that had burdened me all these months. Like a balloon filling slowly with air, becoming all smooth and buoyant, I felt like I finally fit within myself, edge to edge, every crevice filled. (171)

We are so relieved when Haven finally stands tall. A burden has been lifted from us, as well as her.

The unsurprising irony of the height issue rests on the fact that, throughout the novel, others view Haven as a beautiful girl. She gets envious looks from girls at the mall, compliments from Sumner and Ashley, and comments affirming her attractiveness from the elderly women she sees in the senior center where Sumner gives dance lessons. Haven is blind to this truth and assumes that others perceive her as gargantuan, monsterlike, a female Godzilla. Her experience reveals that we define how we see ourselves and are often unaware, even ignorant, as to the perceptions that others hold of us. According to Dessen, the book is "mostly about Haven finding a way to feel comfortable in her skin . . . this idea that confidence can carry you further than you ever could have believed."[7] Haven must first accept herself as she is before she can witness what others see in her.

Relationship Struggles and Joys

There are several thought-provoking relationships to discuss in the context of this novel. Underlying each is the premise that pain is a part of every loving relationship. If we did not care, we would not be saddened or hurt when a meaningful relationship suffers a setback.

The Mother and Daughter

Haven and her mother share a bond that runs deeper than the words either of them can or are willing to express. Dessen captures their relationship in the form of a tether that holds them together even when they are so far apart that the band is close to breaking. In the first scene of the book, we find Haven's mother defrosting the freezer with an ice pick on the morning of her ex-husband's wedding to the weather girl. Haven enters the room to say good morning and fears that her mother will take out an eye as she wipes her brow. She reports:

> I knew that nervous feeling so well, even at fifteen, that spilling uncontrollability that my mother brought out in me. It was as if I was attached to her with a tether, her every movement yanking at me, my own hands reaching to shield her from the dangers of her waving arms. (2)

Later that day, when Haven and Ashley leave for the wedding, the tether pulls at Haven again, willing her to return to her mother who has chosen to stay home. As Haven sees her mother first behind the camera taking photos of her bridesmaid daughters and then again through the screen door on the porch, she feels sad about leaving her behind, abandoning her, when she is certain the experience must be difficult to endure. She chooses not to return to her, however, refusing to face the emotions tied up with the divorce she wishes had never happened and which are confirmed on this wedding day. Throughout the day, Haven cannot shake the memory of her mother and reminisces about her own vision of her parents' simple wedding many years ago, wondering what her mother would think of this fancy church and catered reception. When her father speaks on behalf of her mother, claiming that she certainly wants the girls to be comfortable with his new relationship, Haven gets defensive and does not wish to think of her mother on the day of the start of her father's new life. Despite her loyalties, however, Haven remains unable to offer her mother the comfort she wants to give her. Upon returning home after the festivities, she finds her mother outside working in the garden, her newest distraction since the divorce. Haven has the opportunity to open up to her mother, to provide and gain support and solidarity, but she passes on the chance.

The tether continues to bind Haven, giving her an artificial sense of connection to her mother. She knows her mother well, but only from a distance. On her mother's nights-out with friends, Haven waits until hearing her car in the driveway and key in the door before going to sleep, playing the maternal, protective role. She learns of her mother's concerns and worries indirectly, from her voice carried up from the kitchen through the vent that leads to Haven's bathroom and from the wedding-related sticky notes that seem to have taken over the house. Although Haven wants to pull her mother in and take her away from the world, she refrains from getting too close, as this would mean that she would have to reveal more of herself and make her sadness real. When her mother tells Haven of her potential plans to sell the house, one filled with memories of times when life seemed better, Haven's anger almost leads her to let the dam burst and vent her frustrations. Even still, she sees the concern on her mother's face and keeps silent, choosing to hold back and tuck her emotions inside that hidden and safe part of herself.

It is only when her own life feels out of control that Haven can ignore the urge to protect her mother's fragile emotions or deny her own. Overwhelmed by her sense of loss amidst the changes that surround her, she must let the tether break in order to cope. All of the sadness she has been denying comes forth in the form of anger. When her mother asks her to explain what is bothering her after an episode at work, Haven at first feels that familiar guilt, but she refuses to give in and save her mother any longer. At this point, Haven faces the emotions that she has been suppressing, no longer hiding behind the excuse that she is protecting her mother from the pain of having to discuss or share them. Avoidance is no longer an option. Once Haven accepts this reality, she can stop holding her mother at arm's length and allow her to share in her pain. This new relationship begins to develop on the day of Ashley's wedding. Mother and daughter hold hands as they walk to the car, preparing to create their own memories. More than any protective gesture made toward her mother, Haven's honest admission of anger allows the two to forge a stronger, more honest relationship.

Between Sisters
Haven and Ashley are separated by five years, a fact that becomes more obvious to Haven as her sister plans for her marriage. Now that somber Lewis has entered Ashley's life and seemingly tamed her, Haven misses the sister she remembers from her childhood, the one who played Barbie with her in the driveway after school, painted her toenails during the long summers, and climbed onto the roof with her in the days following the divorce to share in the loss of a father. Now Ashley is concerned solely with details of the wedding and how others perceive her. Through the big event, she attempts to put forth an alternative view of her family from the one held by others—the family that was broken up when the father had an affair with the perky TV girl. Appearances become suddenly very important, something Ashley claims Haven is not yet able to understand.

This lack of understanding is reinforced by the fact that the two sisters differ not only in terms of age but in physical appearance and personality, as well. While Haven is tall, Ashley is petite; while Haven is calm and reserved, Ashley is outgoing and dramatic. Although Ashley, like Haven, has a particular talent for keeping her deepest emotions undercover, Haven is witness to her sister's losses. On the surface, Ashley appears to be in control of her life, ushering new boyfriends in and out of the house. She suffers her heartbreaks in silence, crying herself to sleep on several occasions. The thin walls that divide their rooms, however, give Haven access to her sister's world and allow her to know more about Ashley than Ashley would ever allow. Due to these differences, Haven believes that her sister could never understand her frustrations. More significantly, she fails to give Ashley the chance to hear them, holding her at a distance much as she does with her mother.

This distance and consequential lack of trust result in inaccurate assumptions and subsequent misunderstandings. Haven blames Ashley for setting into motion the changes that are plaguing her life. Once Ashley dumps Sumner, Haven's world begins to fall apart. Because the family is able to keep track of major events based on the young men Ashley has dated, the loss of Sumner equates to the loss of a chapter in life when Haven's happiness was at its perceived peak. Ashley bears the brunt of this false accusation when Haven "chooses" Sumner over her, believing that he was sent away out of habit on the part of Ashley, not knowing that he was the one who cheated on her sister. Ashley is not easy to live with due to her self-centered, bride-to-be behavior, but Haven's inaccurate vision of Sumner (and subsequently Ashley) pushes them farther apart.

Haven has difficulty understanding why Ashley would choose to marry a dolt like Lewis when she could have remained with the contagiously happy Sumner. According to Haven, Ashley shrinks in Lewis' presence, has given up all of the vices that once made her feisty and fun, and has settled for a man who works at the mall and drives a Chevette. When Haven's mother tells her that Ashley is attracted to Lewis because she needs a protective figure due to a lack of father in the house, Haven is even more saddened that her sister would choose someone so unspectacular to take care of her. She admits that Lewis does indeed protect Ashley from old boyfriends, gas station attendants, and bugs, but it is disconcerting to see her spunky sister wither in Lewis' presence.

Haven is surprised to learn that Ashley not only recognizes Haven's feelings toward Lewis but understands them (and her) in a way that she had never anticipated. After Haven learns the truth about Sumner and the way he broke her sister's heart, Ashley confides:

> After Sumner and after Daddy, I was beginning to lose faith in everything. Lewis might not be Sumner, but he would never hurt me. Never. Sometimes things don't turn out the way you want them to, Haven. Sometimes the people you choose to believe are wrong. (192)

With these words, Haven comes to realize that her sister is wiser than she had thought. She might have been consumed by her wedding plans and not as attentive to the needs of her younger sister as she could have been, but she understands the pain of heartbreak and can offer the support that Haven needs now that Haven is learning to trust in her sister and herself. On the day of Ashley's wedding, Haven searches for Ashley, hoping to tell her what she has learned, how she is sorry, how she will miss her, and how she understands Sumner and is grateful that he brought the sisters together again. No words are necessary between sisters, however. Ashley comes down the aisle and, before Haven can speak, leaves her father's side and reaches out to embrace her sister, hugging her, kissing her, telling her that she loves her, showing the insight that Haven had not given her credit for.

The Father and Daughter
Haven and her father, Mac McPhail, share a relationship that embodies the adage that it doesn't hurt if you don't care. Although Haven feels some sadness as a result of her father leaving the family, her pain is due to the fracture in her vision of the ideal family rather than the fact that her father is gone. Even when her father remained with the family, he was absent due to his semi-celebrity status. Haven and her family were forced to compete for his attention. Quite tellingly, Haven states that her mother, before the divorce, spent much of her life "smiling apologetically" while her father "entertained and offended everyone around him" (50). After the divorce, Haven's time spent with her father is awkward and uncomfortable. He refuses to act as though anything has changed and assumes naively that Haven can do the same. Their weekly dinners are spent going through the motions of what a father-daughter experience is supposed to be.

Haven is forced to compete for her father's attention despite the even more limited time she spends with him. She has resigned herself to the fact that she must share her father with the rest of the world. Then and now, time spent with him is time spent with his admiring fans. This truth is evidenced during one of their Thursday evenings out when a fellow sports nut pulls a chair up to the table and begins a long conversation with Mac. The two become so enraptured that Mac fails to notice when Haven leaves the table to use the restroom and doesn't return for quite some time due to a happenstance meeting with Sumner.

Recognizing that the effort required to maintain this relationship is just too much, Haven attempts to make her father accountable by putting the burden of their relationship on him. Each week, until this point, Haven's father pulls up to the house of the enemy and waits, occasionally beeping his horn, but never leaving the safety of his car. Haven puts him to the test when, one evening, she refuses to answer his passive beck and call. He pulls up to the house, beeps twice, and waits. Haven does, too. She wants him to walk up the front steps, across the lawn, and to the front door, to claim her as his own. Mac beeps again and drives off, leaving behind a daughter who feels neither obligated to give him another chance nor deeply saddened by the loss. In challenging her father, Haven accepts the fact that their relationship may not be worth fighting for.

A Supporting Cast

Haven shares relationships with several other characters in her neighborhood and community. Some bring frustration, others humor, and still others powerful insight, but all shape the kind of person that Haven has and will become.

The Widow

Lydia Catrell, the next door neighbor, helps Haven's mother come into her own after the divorce and nurtures a woman Haven has difficulty recognizing at times. An eccentric, Lydia is known for her colorful, often fringed and flashy clothes and huge Lincoln Town Car. She brings out a hidden side of Haven's mother. Much to Haven's surprise, the two go out every Thursday night to Ranzino's, the bar at the Holiday Inn that features oldies music and middle-aged men. Soon after Lydia's arrival, Haven notices the change in her mother. She takes to wearing sandals and sequined shirts, frosting her hair, and pouring her heart out to Lydia at the kitchen table.

As she witnesses these changes, Haven envies the role Lydia now plays in her mother's life. She wishes to be the one across from her at the table, the one with whom her mother shares her deepest confusions and pains regarding the divorce. Although Haven disguises her emotions in the form of envy toward Lydia, her real jealousy is rooted in the fact that her mother is able to move on with her life, to adapt to the changes she has been dealt. Her new interests in gardening, travel, and nights out with a friend leave Haven feeling alone in her sadness. She is the only one who remains in mourning after the break-up of her family. Lydia's arrival and influence on her mother move Haven toward the realization that life goes on.

The Friend
Casey Melvin has been Haven's best friend for years. Casey's high-strung personality is accentuated by the tempestuous love she experiences during summer camp. Upon her return, all she can think about is her painful separation from dear Rick, the boy whose wardrobe she seems to have brought home with her. Casey flounces about in his over-sized shirts in a symbolic attempt to keep him close. Her passion leads her to behave uncharacteristically: running up a long-distance bill; drinking a beer behind the shed during a picnic; taking up smoking; and planning to steal a car and head to Pennsylvania to be reunited with her lover. She becomes paranoid about her mother and believes she is trying to sabotage her relationship with Rick. Fearing that her mother is snooping around her room, Casey sets a trap—individual hairs shut in her dresser drawer and in the latch of her box of important papers.

Although humorous on the surface, these behaviors disappoint Haven who fears that even her dearest friend is changing so significantly that she will soon be unrecognizable. Casey and her new friends inhabit a world so unlike Haven's that she feels she is no longer able to talk with her best friend. The barriers disappear, however, when Rick breaks up with Casey, leaving her hurt and distraught. Haven is the first person Casey calls in her time of need. Despite the gap that has grown between them, Haven reaches out and consoles the girl who, at the core, is still her closest friend. A simple message with profound implications—strong friendships are most valuable when we are weak.

The Model
Gwendolyn Rogers provides an enigmatic comparative character to that of Haven. Gwendolyn is a very tall, very beautiful young woman

who is discovered by an agent during her debut in the Lakeview Mall Model Fashion Show, a small-time operation designed to feature local girls in seasonal attire. She attains celebrity status when she is whisked away to New York and Milan, appears on the cover of *Vogue*, and makes an appearance on *Good Morning America*. Her life seems ideal, many a girl's dream come true.

Although she appears larger than life, however, Gwendolyn's fantasy existence is not so perfect. She is burned in love when she discovers the photographer she adored in bed with another woman—and another man. She returns home the shell of her former self, uncaring about her physical appearance, even timid, so unlike the confident girl who strode down the runways and pouted at the cameras. She spends her days inside and her nights roaming the streets. Haven is fascinated by Gwendolyn's story, not for its sensationalism, but for the sadness of her reality. She wonders about the plausibility of dreams when even those of supermodel and hometown girl Gwendolyn Rogers can be destroyed. Gwendolyn's story, her dream life gone awry, shows Haven that the ideal vision is not always as perfect as we imagine it to be.

In one of the most profound scenes in the novel, Haven and Gwendolyn meet in the woods during a rainstorm, Haven having just fled from Sumner after he fails to live up to her expectations and Gwendolyn taking one of her soul-searching walks. Writing a dream-like sequence, Dessen creates a moment of great power and import. As the two search one another's eyes, with the thunder booming and lightning crashing around them, they see one another in themselves. Haven tells us:

> I wanted to talk to her, wanted words to come so I could say something that would make this all real. Something about what we had in common: a neighborhood, a summer, a revelation about a belief once considered sacred. But she only stared at me, her face wistful, a small smile creeping across it as if she knew me, had lost me along the way and only now found me again, here. I think she knew it too in that moment. She knew me. (189)

While Gwendolyn sees in Haven a reflection of her former self, Haven finds herself.

The Community of Women versus the
Disparateness of Men

Given the engaging and diverse cast of characters in this novel, it is interesting to note that, despite the unique women and men who inhabit
the novel, some patterns relating to gender emerge around them. The
females in *That Summer* share a bond of sisterhood, while the men remain unconnected to others of their gender.

The Women
The women represent the full range of personality types but stand together, respecting and accepting one another even when they may not
like one another. The divorce provides a thought-provoking backdrop
around which to discuss this issue. Haven's family is torn apart when
Lorna enters their lives and steals the patriarch. Although it would be perfectly understandable for Haven's mother, in particular, to remain spiteful
toward Lorna, she faces the situation with a reasonableness that allows for
a sort of forgiveness of her. She recognizes, for example, that the father is
just as, if not more, guilty than Lorna of breaking up the family. On the
morning of Lorna and Mac's wedding, Haven's mother demonstrates her
lack of vindictiveness when she leaves out a newspaper article featuring
the happy couple and their fairy-tale wedding, thus allowing Haven to
read it and make her own judgment about the situation. Although it pains
her to see Lorna and Mac laughing behind their shared desk on the
evening news, she limits her hostility to the Weather Pet nickname.

Lorna, too, recognizes the potential awkwardness of the situation
and tries to maintain civility and a sense of connection. She not only
invites Haven, Ashley, and their mother to the wedding, she sends
them a framed picture of an old family Christmas card that she finds
among Mac's things. Although Haven wonders if this is a demonstra-
tion of poor taste or simply a naive gesture, Lorna's attempt to make
amends and let them know that she recognizes what she has done to
the family is, at least on some level, admirable.

The Men
The men in the novel share no such concern or respect for one another.
There is no community among them. When Haven reintroduces Sum-

ner to her father during one of their weekly dinners, for example, Mac cannot place Sumner in his memory, although he stayed with the family during the summer at Virginia Beach. Haven claims that his gift of selective memory clashes with his eagerness to start over with his new wife, new house, and new memories. Recognizing the risk of applying gender stereotypes, it is interesting that Mac does not hold to his past. Women seem to possess a collective consciousness that spans eons; through birth and death, they are somehow connected to one another. Great-grandmothers have reached through the years to help shape who they are today. Perhaps this explains why the relationship between Haven and her father deteriorates. He is willing to give up the past for the present; she learns to accept the past as a part of her present.

Along the Continuum of Males

In several of her novels, Dessen explores the full range of masculinity, generally celebrating those who reject the most traditional notions of what it means to be a man. *That Summer* provides no exception. In the novel, we are witness to three types of men—the absent, the sweet, and the deceptive.

The Absent
Mac McPhail, Haven's father, fits the bill of the absent man, the father who abandons his children to pursue a life with a younger woman. As mentioned earlier, even when he lives with the family, he is absent, physically and emotionally, due to his semi-celebrity sportscaster status. He knows every "crazy son of a bitch" there is to know, believes in the power of a masculine handshake, and spends his life surrounded by strangers. After the divorce, he is quick to flee, going through the motions of the dutiful father who takes his daughter out to dinner each week. He attempts to spend excessive amounts of money on Haven in place of giving her the time and attention she deserves. When she gives him liberty to exit her life, he accepts readily.

The Sweet
Lewis, in contrast, embodies everything that Mac is not. He is conservative, of few words, respectful, and a neat dresser. He works at the

mall, drives a Chevette, refuses to drink or swear, and, most important, would never hurt Ashley. When she suffers a severe hangover as a result of her bachelorette party the night before, Lewis arrives first thing the next morning with crackers and ginger ale in hand. When he learns that she spent the night at a strip club placing dollar bills in a strange man's G-string, he is shocked and angry, as he takes his vows to Ashley very seriously. Although Haven finds him boring, dry, and without any particularly engaging traits, she recognizes the safety that he provides her sister and believes that his dullness is, in part, what attracted her sister to him in the first place. Lewis may be a peacemaker, a nurturer, even a wimp to some, but he is also a man who is dependable and honest.

The Deceptive
In terms of his role as a male character, Sumner is a bit more difficult to discern. He is ultimately a deceiver, luring Haven into believing he is charming and thoughtful, which, in many ways, he is. Unusual and fascinating things just happen to him, and he is able to make the everyday world seem bizarre and fantastic. Due to the first-person narration of the novel, we must consider Haven's character as we explore any other character. She gives us the lens through which we see those in her world. In the case of Sumner, we need to remember, particularly, that she associates Sumner with an ideal, a summer gone by when her life was perfect, unfettered by change and pain. As a result, Sumner is given special treatment in Haven's portrayal of him. He is enchanting, capable of allowing her to forget, if for just a moment, the reality that she faces when he is away. It is telling, then, when others do not share this perception of Sumner. Despite his active role in her life, Haven's father cannot even place him, and Ashley calls him irresponsible, just a boy, one who hurt her badly. Once Haven learns the truth about Sumner, Ashley reminds her that others are not always as they appear; perception does not always match reality. In this case, Haven's perception is clouded and unreliable. Sumner is indeed a fun character, capable of eliciting laughter, maybe even magic, but, in the end, he chooses to hurt Ashley and, later, Haven. He is not what he seems.

Laughter amid Pain

There are obviously several weighty issues inherent in this text. Despite the seriousness of the themes, however, Dessen has a remarkable capacity to help her characters, and us, keep life in perspective. She uses humor in such a way that we often find ourselves laughing in the most painful, poignant scenes in the book. As narrator, Haven is ultimately responsible for the delivery of this comedic element. To wit, it is through her experiences that we are given cause to laugh. She suffers as a result of the divorce, dreads the impending wedding of her sister, and hates her job at the mall. Yet, it is in the description of these most arduous of experiences that we find ourselves chuckling aloud.

A Funny Divorce?

When Haven relates the tale of the divorce, she incorporates, quite appropriately, weather and news lingo and jargon, resulting in an irony that is painfully funny. She describes her father and Lorna sharing a desk together at work, chatting between themselves at the end of a segment:

> Charlie Baker and Tess Phillips shuffled important-looking papers, worn thin from a hard day of news chasing and news delivering; but my father and the Weather Pet were always off to the side sharing some secret laugh that the rest of us weren't in on. And when we finally did catch on, it wasn't very funny after all. (3)

Haven remembers sitting in front of the television each night watching her father and Lorna exchange looks before commercial breaks, clueless to the fact that the two were planning their new life together. A woman, known for her "short skirts and pouty-lipped way of saying 'upper-level disturbance,'" would soon come between Haven and her seemingly ideal past when "Rowdy Ron the Weather Mon, who was overweight, more than a little crazy, and no threat to [her] parents' marriage whatsoever" (11, 59) still did the weather.

Wedding Bliss?

Planning for Ashley's wedding fails to offer a diversion to Haven's sadness. It does, however, demonstrate how preparing for a wedding can be anything but blissful. In addition to Ashley's bad-bride behavior, late-night planning meetings, and a home filled with sticky note reminders of things that need to be attended to, Haven and her family must contend with Carol Cliffordson, a distant cousin to Haven and Ashley who spent one summer with them when they were younger. Carol and Ashley, both twelve, were inseparable, and, although they have not spent any time together since, Ashley insists on having her as a bridesmaid. Carol turns out to be a problem. She first objects to the low-cut dress that Ashley wishes for her to wear, due, of course, to the fact that she is rather flat-chested. She then calls to say she will be unable to attend the ceremony because her fiancé's family members will be in town that same weekend and want her to participate in the annual cookout and square dance. Although Carol is persuaded to come anyway, fiancé in tow, and leave immediately after the ceremony, this solution does not hold. The process continues on-again, off-again until, in the end when the wedding finally arrives, there is a gap where Carol would have been, symmetry be damned.

Dream Job?

Haven cannot even find respite in her work. She spends her summer vacation working for a stodgy man named Burt Isker, pushing socks as an impulse purchase at the orders of corporate headquarters, removing shoes from the feet of grubby little kids, forcing cheap and ugly shoes on their parents, and handing out listless, helium-free balloons. The highlight of her summer work experience is in her viewing of the annual Lakeview Mall Models Fall Spectacular, a fashion show designed to feature back-to-school clothes available at stores in the mall. This year, spectators enjoy more than the one lone ficus tree that served as a single prop the year before. The new director's vision entails disco music with a quick beat and the sound of a woman panting, colored lights and glitter, and models dressed in torn jeans and combat boots, a far cry from the plaid jumpers and nice sweaters the mothers in the audience have come to expect. Dessen helps us to remember that everyday life is funny.

With the publication of *That Summer*, Dessen introduced unwittingly her voice into the realm of young adult literature. Hers is a distinct and welcome voice, one that, in this first novel, captures gracefully and honestly the realities of teenage life despite being written with adult readers in mind. Given the originally intended audience, Dessen's writing style is rich and often eloquent without being lofty, and her story possesses a depth and style that move readers beyond the formulaic teen love story. Ironically, perhaps the complexities of Dessen's stories are just what young readers crave, as hers is a voice that speaks from experience and from the heart.

Notes

1. Review of *That Summer*, by Sarah Dessen, *Kirkus Reviews*, 15 September 1996.

2. Hazel Rochman, review of *That Summer*, by Sarah Dessen, *Booklist*, 15 October 1996, 422.

3. Rochman, *Booklist*.

4. Nancy Vakilakis, review of *That Summer*, by Sarah Dessen, *The Horn Book*, November/December 1996, 742.

5. Vakilakis, *The Horn Book*.

6. *Kirkus Reviews*.

7. Sarah Dessen, "*That Summer*," *Personal Website*, at www.sarahdessen.com/thatsummer.html (accessed 4 March 2003).

~

CHAPTER FOUR

Needing *Someone Like You* to Figure Out Me

"Life is an ugly, awful place to not have a best friend" (1). Dessen's second novel, *Someone Like You* (1998), is about friendship, the kind of friendship that sees us through the surprising, the painful, the seemingly impossible. The story is dedicated to Bianca, Dessen's best friend from high school, the girl who, in Dessen's words, "was there firsthand for all the real truths of us trying to survive high school, and knows even the stories I don't tell."[1] Drawn partially from the death of a popular boy during Dessen's ninth-grade year, the novel explores universal themes—best friends, first loves, overbearing parents—and the thread that binds true friends together as they move through the changing nature of these relationships.

Dessen claims that this novel was difficult to write, in part due to the success that her first novel, *That Summer*, enjoyed. The pressure to create an equally strong or stronger story weighed on her, as did the arduous editing process that resulted from her tendency to include more details than necessary and repeat herself. The novel "more than fulfills the promise of her first book,"[2] however, and has been well-received by young readers and critics alike. Among her novels, *Someone Like You* has "the biggest legion of fans,"[3] and Dessen receives regular email requests from readers asking her to continue the story of Halley and Scarlett in a future book. The novel was named winner of the 2001 South

Carolina Young Adult Book Award, 2001 Missouri Gateway Book Award, and the Maryland Library Association Black-Eyed Susan Award; was selected by the American Library Association as a Best Book for Young Adults and a Quick Pick for Reluctant Readers; and was cited as a *School Library Journal* Best Book of the Year and barnesandnoble.com Top Ten Teen Novel.

Named after her independent grandmother and the famous comet, Halley, the novel's protagonist, tries to find her sense of self as she journeys through her junior year of high school. The tumultuous ride begins with the death of Michael, a classmate and first love of Scarlett, Halley's best friend, and the unexpected news that Scarlett is pregnant with Michael's child. Halley's life is complicated further by the ever-increasing gap that develops between her and her mother, a therapist who has made her name touting the healthy relationship she shares with her daughter. The canyon becomes wider when Halley meets and falls for Macon, a rebellious young man who runs with the wild crowd, is not burdened by parental expectations, and eventually lets her down. Amidst these forces—the maintenance of a friendship during a difficult time, the pride and pain of asserting herself against her mother's pull, and the rush and heartbreak of first love—Halley must choose the kind of girl she hopes to be. Although others influence her life and her world, her destiny is hers to decide.

A Problem Novel

Fiction for adolescents has a long and sordid history of being didactic and preachy. Considering the impressionable age of the intended audience, young adult authors have attempted, on occasion, to impart a worthy moral message in hopes of influencing readers to make correct choices given the time and social milieu in which the work is written. Books put into print by the American Sunday School Union in the early 1800s serve as telling examples. In this fiction, two plot patterns were generally followed: "A young child near death would remind readers of all his virtues, all that they must remember and practice, and then the child would die, to the relief of readers," or stories would describe "good children who had temporarily forgotten duties to parents and siblings and who would soon get their comeuppance."[4] Domestic novels which followed a few decades later and had a female audience in mind maintained the tradition of didacticism. The domestic novel "preached morality; woman's submission to man; the value of cultural, social, and political conservatism; a religion of the heart and the Bible; and the glories of suffering."[5] Both genres attempted to teach right versus wrong as dictated by the dominant culture's value system.

Considering its inclusion of a teen pregnancy, *Someone Like You* could have fallen easily into the same pattern. We could have been led to feel sorry for Scarlett, to pity her and her condition. Dessen's portrayal of Scarlett, however, gives us the image of a strong, capable young woman who, in facing difficult circumstances, demonstrates the maturity and conviction of a responsible, caring human being. She fights to keep her baby even though her mother hopes she will give up the child for adoption, changes her eating and exercise habits when she learns this will benefit the baby, and braves the stares that follow her at school and at work. She has made her choice, and she will stick with it, a truth that causes Halley to wonder "why the right thing always seemed to be met with so much resistance, when you'd think it would be the easier path. You had to fight to be virtuous" (200). Dessen says that she was not trying to convey a political message in her choice to have Scarlett keep the child. Instead, she was working to develop a realistic character. In speaking of Scarlett's decision, she says, "No, it's not normal. No, it's not the choice everyone should make, but, for Scarlett, nothing in her life has been normal up until this point. She's already been a mother to her own mother for all these years in a lot of ways, and this is just what she is going to do."

By being candid about the realities of sex, pregnancy, and childbirth, Dessen much more convincingly, and perhaps ironically, dissuades young readers from jumping into a sexual relationship for which they are ill-prepared physically and emotionally. Adolescent readers, females in particular, will "appreciate the book's honest explication of the things they really want to know."[6] Sexual myths are exposed and glossy images of beaming pregnant women are called into question, forcing young readers to confront the realities of what they might face should they decide to become sexually active. When Scarlett reveals to Halley that she is pregnant, she explains that she and Michael used protection but that the condom somehow came off and that she did not imagine she could get pregnant as a result of having sex the first time. Halley admits that she, too, is unclear about the logistics of sex and cannot explain how this could have happened to her responsible friend. As the pregnancy advances, readers are exposed to "the discomfort and the drag," as well as the mysteries and joys of carrying a child. A pregnancy book becomes their pseudo-Bible as the girls figure out how to deal with Scarlett's increasing moodiness, aversion to foods, and morning sickness. Scarlett encapsulates her experience in the claim, "Whenever I used to see pregnant women, they always looked happy. Glowing, right? Or on TV, in those big dresses, knitting baby afghans. No one ever tells you it makes you fat and sick and crazy" (137). Scarlett fears, too, what she will face in the delivery room, not to mention what she will experience as a young mother. A visit to the doctor does nothing to calm her worries, as the physician is supportive, but frank. She tells Scarlett that, although there are techniques designed to lessen the pain and that millions of women have had children and lived to tell about it, the birth process will hurt. This is confirmed when Scarlett finds herself in the delivery room, experiencing contractions that cause her to go pale in the face and emit an animal-like, guttural groan that elicits great fear in Halley, her birthing partner. There is no glamour here.

Watching Scarlett deal with the consequences of pregnancy forces Halley to consider her own readiness for sex. As Macon pushes Halley to sleep with him, promising her that they will be careful, she begins to question whether or not the act is as big a deal as she believed. She fears losing Macon and knows that he will leave her if she does not give in to him soon. In the back of her mind, however, is the vision of Scarlett who was being careful, too. Halley tells Scarlett that sex is just something that guys like Macon do. Scarlett reminds Halley that the decision is not one for Macon to make. "If you sleep with him," she warns, "it will change things. . . . It has to. And if he goes, you'll have lost more than just him" (187). As Halley ponders her decision, Scarlett's words remain with her, but Macon's urgings are seemingly too strong. Halley promises Macon that she will sleep with him on New Year's Eve, even though she admits to herself that the decision does not feel right. When she finds herself lying on a dirty bed in a run-down house in the middle of a drunken party about to give herself away to a young man who has not yet told her he loves her, she chooses sensibly to walk away, even though this means a sure end to her relationship with Macon. Although it is not an easy decision, Halley holds true to her beliefs and gives readers a realistic model to emulate. Halley is no prude. She experiences pleasure as she and Macon explore one another's bodies. At times, it is difficult for her to pull away; the physical urge is so strong. Readers will appreciate the reality of these sensations and emotions. Halley is imperfect, tempted, and, ultimately, wise.

Friendship

Halley and Scarlett's shared relationship allows them to remain strong as individuals even when they feel most weak. Halley is used to Scarlett being the bolder, the braver of the two, the one who chased off the toughest of the pesky girls who ruled the neighborhood as they rode around on their fancy pink bikes. She is the one who stands by Halley when it seems that Macon has stood her up for their first date, telling her, "Any guy would be damn lucky to have you, Halley, and you know it. You're beautiful and smart and loyal and funny. . . . You're special" (80). She is the one who talks frankly with Halley as she considers whether or not to have sex with Macon. She tells Halley what she needs to hear even when Halley feels that Scarlett is being disloyal and untrusting.

Scarlett embodies the kind of girl that Dessen gravitated toward during her own childhood, the girl who is more outspoken and outgoing than herself. She claims that her girlfriends were (and are) "smart and gorgeous and fearless" and that she never sees herself as possessing any of these traits.[7] It is telling, however, that Halley steps up when Scarlett most needs her, demonstrating the resourcefulness and courage that she (and perhaps Dessen) so often attributes to and admires in others. When she first visits Scarlett after learning of Michael's death, Halley is lost as to what she should do, as Scarlett is usually the consoler in their relationship. Halley remembers Scarlett's response to the many tears she has shed on her capable friend's shoulder and follows her lead, wrapping her arms around Scarlett, having no idea what should come next, but knowing that this is the best she can do. Even before this emotional event, Halley supports Scarlett's happiness even though it sometimes makes her sad. Once Michael enters Scarlett's life, Halley inevitably sees less of her friend. Although she sometimes feels as though she has to fight for Scarlett's attention, she witnesses her friend's happy glow and almost ever-present laughter and holds nothing against her.

Scarlett's pregnancy provides the most obvious opportunity for Halley to shine as a friend. Although she is frightened as to what the next nine months and beyond will entail, she views it as her job to hold herself and Scarlett together. It is now her turn to offer the support she has so often received from Scarlett. She drives Scarlett to her doctor's appointments, helps her price cribs and strollers, takes her out late at night to satisfy ice cream cravings, helps her draft a letter to Michael's mother revealing the existence of the baby, defends her against petty attacks from her peers, and attends Lamaze classes with her. She is the one Scarlett calls for when she goes into labor at the prom; she is the one Scarlett has come to depend upon.

Halley's strength is tested when the delivery process begins. Although she promises Scarlett that she will not leave her side, Scarlett's frightened response to labor leads Halley to lose her cool. She feels in over her head, unable to handle the moment now that it has arrived. She leaves the room despite Scarlett's pleas for her to stay, leans against the door, and feels as though she is falling apart. It is Halley's mother who reminds her of the responsibility true friendship requires. She arrives on the scene and tells Halley that Scarlett is counting on her, that she is the only one she wants by her side as she delivers the child. Halley's support matters to Scarlett, as evidenced when she reveals that the name of the new baby will be Grace Halley, named for her dearest friend. Friendships are important in life. Dessen gets is right when she says:

> I learned early on that your girlfriends are sometimes the only people you can really rely on when things get sticky. I always think that I get the best parts of myself from what my friends have taught me about strength and loyalty and spirit. Plus, they make me laugh, still, and remind me where I've come from even as I'm so focused on where I'm going.[8]

Mothers and Daughters

There are two mother-daughter pairs of interest in the novel, the one comprised of Halley and Julie and the other of Scarlett and Marion. Although the relationships between mother and daughter differ considerably, adult and child find a way to coexist.

Self-Reliance through Vulnerability

Halley and Julie struggle to find their way as their relationship shifts. Not so long ago, Halley and Julie considered themselves best friends. Halley felt as though she could tell her mother anything. She remembers sitting at the kitchen table after school each day, waiting for her mother's car to pull up so she could share the latest news. After Halley's first dance, mother and daughter shared every detail over ice cream, and each Saturday, they enjoyed lunch out together so that they could stay caught up with one another. Halley is proud of her mother's strength and ability to solve most any dilemma. Julie, too, takes great pride in the relationship she shares with her daughter, writing journal articles, speaking with parents at school, and chatting with her friends about the success she has enjoyed in the raising of her daughter. As a reminder of their strong bond, she keeps a framed photograph of mother and daughter, happy in one another's company, posing together during a family vacation at the Grand Canyon.

At the start of the summer, however, this bond strains under the pressure of Halley's desire for independence. The canyon begins to widen as Halley strives to move from vulnerable daughter to self-reliant woman. Halley starts her first job, spends time with wild Ginny Tabor, and breaks up with Noah, the childhood friend her mother hopes she will marry. Halley is tired of her mother having a hand in everything she does, from being expected to watch movies and eat popcorn with Noah and his family, as has been done every Friday night for years, to determining the company she is and is not allowed to keep. Julie even insists that Halley's memory of the comet that she and her grandmother watched together is inaccurate. It was too hazy to see anything at all, she claims. The assertiveness that Halley once admired in her mother has become an obstacle to her own growth.

This conflict comes to a head when Julie learns of Macon's role in her daughter's life. She demands, completely within character, that Halley no longer see him and assumes without question that her demand will be met. Halley feels like a pawn in a game over which she has no control:

> I sat there and looked at my mother, at the ease in her face as she told me how I felt, what I thought, everything. Like I was a puzzle, one she'd created, and she knew the solution every time. If she couldn't keep me close to her, she'd force me to be where she could always find me. (170)

Although Halley views her mother's behavior as manipulative and controlling, Julie acts out of a maternal desire to protect her daughter. She does not want Halley to get hurt. In denying Halley the right to make her own choices, however, she refuses to let her daughter learn on her own and develop the sense of reliance that Halley so admires (and is so frustrated by) in her mother. Halley proves to her mother, however, that she deserves to be able to take the risk. After rejecting Macon, Halley returns to the house to find her mother waiting for her. Julie presumes that Halley has snuck out to see Macon and immediately lectures her about the poorness of her choices. Halley confronts her mother, telling her that she will never learn unless her mother lets her. Choices leave us vulnerable, but, unless we can make our own choices, we can never become strong. Halley's stand leads to a turning point in their relationship. She tells us, "And so we stood there in the kitchen, my mother and I, facing off over everything that had built up since June, when I was willing to hand myself over free and clear. Now, I needed her to return it all to me, with the faith that I could make my own way" (245). Although the process has just begun, Halley glimpses her mother biting her tongue every now and then, as she learns a new way to interact with her daughter and give her the freedom she needs.

Halley, too, must learn to see her mother in a new light for their relationship to move forward. Halley envisions her mother as completely in control of her own life (and often those of others). Julie maintains a professional voice even when awakened at 1:30 in the morning, maintains a neighborly smile and wave while in the midst of an argument with Halley, and is able to negotiate peace between Scarlett and Marion when the pregnancy is revealed. Julie is strong, but she is also human, capable of sadness and pain and a sense of loss. This side of her mother is revealed as Julie faces the illness of her own mother. Halley witnesses her mother as a daughter. On a visit to the hospital, she sees Julie, who has spent the entire visit reassuring Halley that all will be fine, crying at her mother's bedside. Halley is frightened by this image, revealing, "There are some things in this world you rely on, like a sure bet. And when they let you down, shifting from where you've carefully placed them, it shakes your faith, right where you stand" (197). There is more to Julie than what Halley has assumed; she, too, is vulnerable. Halley comes to realize that her mother is an essential part of herself. Although she wishes to be her own person, her mother, both self-reliant and vulnerable, is, in part, responsible for that person. When Julie forces Halley to return to Scarlett's side during the birth and remains to offer whispered words of support, Halley accepts her mother as a part of her, as necessary as her own heart, regardless of how much she wishes to break away.

Peace through Acceptance

The relationship between Scarlett and Marion embodies the reversal of role expectation; mother behaves as daughter and vice versa. Since she was five years old, Scarlett has been the primary caregiver to her mother, a woman who is unlike any that Halley has known. Marion, a recovering alcoholic, reads *Vogue*, wears revealing clothes, chain-smokes, has a closet of great envy to any fashion guru, and regularly brings home men to whom Scarlett says goodbye the next morning. Scarlett has spent her life cleaning up after her mother, tidying the house, washing the dishes, paying the bills, and getting help when her mother is passed out on the front walk. These roles seem to work for the two. Although they are not close, they live together amicably, each accepting her place in the relationship.

Tension arises, however, with the discovery of Scarlett's pregnancy. Marion takes the news as an attack on her ability as a mother, believing that this proves she has been a poor maternal example. Although Scarlett does not hold this view, Marion changes her ways in an endeavor to make amends for the kind of mother she has been. She attempts to assert control over her daughter, demanding that Scarlett have an abortion. When Scarlett, used to making her own choices, opts to keep the baby instead, their relationship is in peril. It is only through the intervention of Halley's mother that Scarlett does not run away from home and abandon her mother. Upon Scarlett's decision to not only keep the baby but raise it as her own, Marion alters her tactics and encourages adoption. She leaves brochures and pamphlets throughout the house in hopes of influencing Scarlett. By this point, however, it is too late. Scarlett has already learned to be independent and strong; she is not willing to relinquish her dominant role in the relationship. Marion's position was established long ago. She must, and eventually does, accept Scarlett's wishes and embrace willingly her daughter and her daughter's daughter. Halley witnesses this acceptance when she sees Marion standing alone in the newly-prepared nursery, smiling.

Searching for the Self

Halley's quest for her identity is bound up with her relationships with her mother and Macon. For most of her early life, Halley assumes the role of quiet, mousy girl who chooses bossy friends who push her around and send her home to her waiting mother. Halley likens her view of herself to that of an outline in a coloring book, the inside as yet incomplete; "the colors, the zigzags and plaids, the bits and pieces" (23) that define Halley are not yet visible. During the summer before her junior year, however, Halley is ready to explore the New Her, to experiment with the kind of girl she might wish to become. This process begins when she spends time with wild Ginny—taking up the habits of smoking, drinking, tanning, and piercing—and breaks up with good old Noah. With these choices, she begins to drift away from the girl her mother expects her to be, a progression Halley relishes. She is tired of being the perfect daughter.

The arrival of Macon gives Halley further opportunity to establish her independence from her mother and provide the interior of her outline some color. She feels like a different person when she is with Macon, free to play along as if she is as wild as he, to imagine herself as a carefree girl with no parents looking over her shoulder. She lets Macon assume that she is out late at night when she is really safe at home abiding by her curfew and acts as though she knows of the parties he describes even though she is clueless. With Macon, she can be the bold and reckless girl that he believes her to be, living vicariously through the casual details of his rebellious existence that he throws out in their conversations during P.E. class.

Halley's actions soon begin to match her vision when she begins to take on the characteristics of the wild girl she wishes to become. She claims she is willing to do anything Macon asks, even if it is dangerous. She lies to her parents about how she spends her Friday nights, ditches school, and sneaks out on her birthday, all actions that arouse in her an intoxicating mix of guilt and pleasure. She hates to deceive her parents, but the world looks so different, so fresh, so new when she is with Macon. His mysterious ways are too intriguing to pass up. When he kisses her, she feels the girl from the Grand Canyon slipping away; she willingly lets go. When she sees her reflection in the mirror, she sees "the girl who belonged with Macon Faulkner, the girl who broke her mother's heart, never looking back" (161).

Despite her new vision of self, however, Halley has not yet come into her own. While she was once Halley, Scarlett's friend, she is now Halley, Macon's girlfriend. She is not yet just Halley. Even Halley realizes that she is living a role that does not suit her. Halley is not foolish, only intentionally blind. She is aware that Macon has little regard for her home situation, despite the fact that it causes her much angst. He calls late at night and squeals his tires as he tears down the road, leaving her to deal with her mother's anger and frustration. She realizes, too, that his desire for sex will be fulfilled elsewhere if she chooses not to give in and that he does not understand why giving up this part of herself is so significant to her. She wonders if Macon belongs with someone else or, more significantly, if she does not belong with him. She wonders if he loves her but already knows the answer.

Her wonderings cease on the night she plans to sleep with Macon. While she rests on the dirty bed in the dirty house feeling dirty inside, Halley accepts that she has been wrong. She does not belong here or with Macon. As she flees the room, she finds herself afraid and angry—at Macon, at herself, and at Scarlett and her mother for being right about her relationship with Macon. Macon catches up with her and escorts her home, but he is so angry and frustrated with her that he drives recklessly, runs a red light, puts Halley in the hospital, and never bothers to visit. As she recovers, Halley finds the strength to see the truth about Macon. When he comes to her bedroom window seeking forgiveness, she sees him without his magical façade and is no longer impressed.

She wants and deserves more. It is time to begin her own journey rather than follow the lead of someone else—mother, friend, or boyfriend. Although she does not know what Halley will eventually be, she is ready to embark upon the process of becoming.

The Gender Gap

As in Dessen's other novels, the opposing roles between women and men are evidenced in *Someone Like You*. While the women are portrayed as strong, even in their weakest moments, the men remain on the periphery, "only there as background."[9]

Strong Women

The women in the novel grow and develop over the course of the story, becoming stronger, more admirable people as a result. As discussed above, Halley rejects her second-hand status and comes to understand her importance as a human being, one capable of making of herself that which she will, and Julie, Halley's mother, becomes a better mother when she learns to respect and trust her daughter. Scarlett's mother, Marion, may not be the most admirable of parents, but she, too, demonstrates a tenacity that hints at her ability to see herself through difficult times and emerge alive, although a bit bruised. While a senior in high school, she finds herself pregnant with Scarlett. When the father, football player and student council president, goes away to school, Marion refuses to contact him and attempts to raise Scarlett alone, a choice Scarlett labels the most unselfish thing her mother could have done. Although Marion struggles with Scarlett's decision to keep the baby, fearing that her daughter may suffer the same difficulties as she did, she eventually comes to respect Scarlett's decision. Scarlett's strength is confirmed when she makes her decision and sticks with it. Despite her fears about labor and delivery and sadness over the death of Michael, she puts her baby first and perseveres even when she feels lost and incapable, tired and alone. In the end, all of the women unite, "all strong and loving together for their newborn girl,"[10] ready to give little Grace the individual gifts they have to share—Scarlett's spirit, Julie's strength, Marion's determination, and Halley's wisdom.

Peripheral Men

In stark contrast, the men remain stagnant, on the outside looking in, failing to grow or develop or be changed by the world around them. Macon learns nothing from his experience with Halley. After the accident, he utters his practiced and hollow claim of love, just as he has pronounced the words to hundreds of other girls in his past. He quickly takes up with another shortly after the break-up. He continues his rebellious behavior—rarely attending school, living a nomadic existence as he moves from home to home of whomever will have him for a time, remaining accountable to no one.

The singular role of Halley's father is to provide comic relief. He is amused by the fact that some high school kids have altered the sign that sits outside their housing development from a Neighborhood of Friends to a Neighborhood of Fiends, and he relishes the fact that his yard is considered close to impossible to tend, even with the use of The Beast, his prized lawn mower. A local disc jockey, he spends his days telling booger jokes, performing stunts due to lost on-air bets, and wrestling a man named the Dominator for charity. When conflict develops between Halley and her mother, he is the placater, the one who says nothing during the dispute but brings Halley chocolate milkshakes as a peace offering. He is boyishly sweet but takes no active part in helping his daughter become more independent. In fact, he encourages her rash behavior. When Halley's mother must leave town to care for her own mother, he leaves Halley free to spend time with Macon, even though her mother has declared him off limits. Both father and daughter know she is getting away with murder, but the dad refuses to step in and take any responsibility.

Michael, the father of Scarlett's baby, sets events in motion and disappears. We never have the opportunity to see whether or not he will become altered in the course of the story. Although Michael cannot be blamed for the accident, Dessen's decision to eliminate him from the narrative is essential to Scarlett's development. In terms of plot structure, his absence requires that Scarlett face her situation without knowing what might have been. Based on what she knew of him in his life, she is forced to speculate how their future would have looked. While alive, Michael is beloved by all, a part of no particular social group but befriended by each. He is charming in his courtship of Scarlett, leaving various fruits as tokens of his affection at the grocery store register where she works as a clerk. A prankster, a great storyteller, a bit magical, Michael remains an enigma, on the outside, but key to the story. Scarlett recognizes, however, that he might not have maintained this persona upon learning of his impending fatherhood. She admits that she knew him only a short time and accepts that he might have turned out to be a jerk just as easily as he might have been the one to help her through.

Even Cameron, the most admirably portrayed male in the story, fails to move forward in his development. He is the new boy in school, the one with the pasty skin and completely black wardrobe, the one with the funny accent acquired during his studies in France, the artistic and quirky one befriended by Scarlett. He is a nurturer who thanks Scarlett by taking care of her during the pregnancy—rubbing her feet, making her cookies, and painting the nursery. He is the antithesis to all things traditionally masculine. Yet, he is unable to maintain his subtle strength at the most crucial time, during the labor and delivery of Scarlett's baby. He has been preparing for the moment for months, and, when it arrives, he is unable to rise to the occasion. He almost passes out at the prom when Scarlett begins to labor and remains in the waiting room while she endures the process. When he has the chance to enlarge himself through his experiences, he shrinks.

Humor on the Sidelines

Amid the struggles of pregnancy, strained relationships, and personal development, Dessen manages to keep things light through the inclusion of one of the most intriguing, bizarre, and endearing characters in her novels—Steve Michaelson, the man Marion is currently dating. Although his role in the novel is not central, his presence is strongly felt. Steve, an accountant during the week, spends his weekends performing as a member of a medieval period club. He and his friends dress up in medieval attire, assume alter-egos, and joust and sing at tournaments and festivals of their creation. In the creation of this character, Dessen was inspired by an experience of her own youth when she used to hang out at a restaurant frequented by members of the Society for Creative Anachronism. She remembers sitting there sipping her Coke, fascinated by the group members' regalia and courage to demonstrate such commitment to a hobby.

In and of itself, the group's behavior is unusual, perhaps, but not truly funny. It is the gradual unveiling of Steve's medieval self in the midst of his modern day life that leads to passages of laugh-aloud humor. When we are first introduced to Steve, he seems a mild-mannered, polite, rather quiet man who is (and remains) respectful and proper in his dealings with Marion. When he arrives in his Hyundai hatchback, flowers in hand, nothing seems amiss. As his relationship with Marion develops, however, clues as to his alternate identity, that of Vlad the Warrior (or the Impaler, as Scarlett likes to call him), are revealed. Around the third or fourth date, he arrives wearing not only his usual tie, oxford shirt, sports jacket, dress pants, and loafers with tassels but a large, circular medallion with unusual symbols and words inscribed within. Although Marion insists it is only a piece of jewelry, Scarlett argues that it is instead a weird warrior coin. She claims that "his other side can't be held down any longer. It's starting to push out of him, bit by bit" (146). Soon thereafter come the boots. Not regular boots, but warrior boots, "big, leather, clunky boots with a thick heel and buckles" that clank loudly with each step, "poking out from beneath his pants leg as if they'd just walked over the heads of dead opponents" (171–72). The revealing does not end here. Next comes the tunic (still worn with dress pants). Finally, the transformation is complete when he arrives clad in his medallion, boots, tunic, burlap pants, a kind of cape, carrying a sword on his hip. He stands next to the spice rack in Marion's home, "a living anachronism" (222). He is so empassioned in his hobby that he ultimately convinces Marion to join him; she claims it is nice to pretend to be someone else every once in a while. We can relate to Steve's (Vlad's) escapist tendencies, as life is not always amusing on its own.

Someone Like You is so much more than a book about teenage pregnancy. Scarlett's experiences are important, but this is Halley's story. It is Halley who struggles to maintain a friendship, maneuver through her first love, define herself as more than someone's daughter, and figure out who she wants to be. Scarlett's pregnancy provides a backdrop against which to monitor Halley's growth. As Dessen describes, "The pregnancy goes in tandem with Halley coming into her own. When the baby is born, Halley is reborn." She is a new girl, her own girl.

Notes

1. Sarah Dessen, *"Someone Like You," Personal Website*, at www.sarahdessen.com/someone.html (accessed 4 March 2003).

2. Nancy Vasilakis, review of *Someone Like You*, by Sarah Dessen, *The Horn Book*, July/August 1998, 486.

3. Dessen, *"Someone Like You," Personal Website*.

4. Alleen Pace Nilsen and Kenneth L. Donelson, *Literature for Today's Young Adults*, 6th ed. (New York: Longman, 2001), 45.

5. Nilsen and Donelson, *Literature*, 49.

6. Vasilakis, *The Horn Book*.

7. "An Interview with Sarah Dessen," *DreamGirl Magazine*, at www.dgarts.com/content/saradessen.htm (accessed 4 March 2003).

8. "An Interview with Sarah Dessen," *DreamGirl Magazine*.

9. Hazel Rochman, review of *Someone Like You*, by Sarah Dessen, *Booklist*, 1 June 1998, 1745.

10. Rochman, *Booklist*.

CHAPTER FIVE

∼

Keeping the Moon and Giving In to the Mystery of It All

"It is what it is" (35). In her third novel, *Keeping the Moon* (1999), Dessen encourages the acceptance of self, noting the power that personal perception holds over one's self-concept and sense of identity. What we believe about ourselves weighs more heavily than an external reality or the views of others. When we are confident and trust in who we are, this power of perception allows us to be strong even when others see us as weak. When we see ourselves as less than we are, however, we allow a faulty perception to determine our reality, and even the most flattering of compliments will not alter our vision of self unless we are willing to make this change. It is only when we look within to determine who we really are, matching perception to reality, that we find the freedom to become what we will. Others may assume, but we determine the truth about who we are.

This message is close to Dessen's heart. Like Colie, her fifteen-year-old narrator, Dessen is still trying to learn the lessons about confidence and self-esteem that the novel contains. She hopes readers will learn that "it's what is inside that gets you where you are truly meant to be."[1] Written while Dessen worked as a waitress at the Flying Burrito (and dedicated to past and present dancing burritogirls everywhere), the novel is grounded in experiences about which Dessen speaks firsthand. Like Colie, she, too, had a customer reply with a sardonic, "Duh," when

Dessen revealed she was new on the job. Like Morgan, Colie's mentor waitress, she consoles herself with devilled eggs when times are difficult. And, like us all, she is still learning what it means to find herself in the midst of work, relationships, and life. The combination of the novel's universal themes and Dessen's skill as a storyteller has led to a critically acclaimed work of fiction. Selected as an American Library Association Best Book for Young Adults, an American Library Association Quick Pick for Reluctant Readers, a New York Public Library Book for the Teen Age, an International Reading Association Young Adult Choice, and a *School Library Journal* Best Book of the Year, the work has been defined as "rich in sharply observed relationships, deftly inserted wisdom, romances ending and beginning, and characters who are not afraid to pick themselves up and try again," leaving readers to feel "thoughtful, amused, reassured, and sorry when it concludes."[2]

Colie is used to being an outcast. She is first shunned by her peers for being overweight and then, once the weight is lost, for her reputation for being easy. Although she sheds her excess pounds, she is unable to shake her sense of insecurity and lack of confidence brought on by the perceptions of others. While her mother, fitness guru Kiki Sparks, embarks on her European Summer FlyKiki Fitness Tour, Colie spends her vacation in Colby, North Carolina, with her lively, eccentric Aunt Mira. Through a twist of fate, she finds herself working as a waitress with her next door neighbors, twenty-somethings Morgan and Isabel, at the Last Chance Bar and Grill. These two new friends force Colie to come out from behind her dyed black hair, lip ring, and surly attitude. Under their nurturing care (and that of Mira, Kiki, and Norman, the young artist who lives downstairs and eventually steals her heart), Colie learns to see in herself that which she never knew existed deep within her all along.

The Danger and Power of Assumptions

Colie falls victim to false assumptions that others hold about her. She is first plagued by her weight, suffering the taunts and jeers of her classmates who label her "fat ass," "lard-o," and "thunder thighs." Her peers refuse to get to know her because of her physical appearance, heightened perhaps by the persona she puts forth as a result of her belief that others will not accept her. A self-fulfilling prophecy is at work here. At her first school dance, she is humiliated when one of the popular boys imitates her moves on the dance floor, making a mockery of her large size and leading onlookers to stare at her and laugh. She is not even welcome among other overweight students because her mother's travels make her the perpetual new kid as she moves from school to school. With Kiki's success, Colie and her mother can afford to buy a home in a nice neighborhood and remain settled. Even so, the isolation and loneliness continue. During gym class, Colie's large underwear is put on display, one of the many pranks she suffers as a result of her appearance. As the overweight daughter of Kiki Sparks, her suffering is compounded. How must a fitness expert feel about having a fat daughter?

Yet even when Colie sheds forty-five-and-a-half pounds, reclaiming muscles and taut skin that were hidden from view, the hurt of the old labels remains, and more false associations are assigned. Once the weight is gone, her peers simply shift tactics, manipulating the truth and spreading rumors that Colie is easy, a "Hole-in-One." Due to her lack of self-confidence, Colie is an easy target. Her response to this treatment is to create a shell around herself, to distance herself so the eyes and voices of others cannot penetrate her skin. She gets her lip pierced, cuts her hair with nail scissors and dyes it red, dates a boy who wants nothing more from her than a good time, and loses herself in loud music to drown her sorrow.

No longer hindered by the views of those from her past, Colie hopes to begin again and create a fresh identity in Colby. She knows the pain that can result from false assumptions. Ironically, however, she bases her perceptions of her new acquaintances upon surface glances, first impressions, and quickly-made judgments. To avoid making meaningful connections and potentially getting hurt, she clings to a limited understanding of those around her, believing she knows these people better than she really does. Her perceptions of others are rooted in the assumptions others have made about her, which she has allowed to shape her identity. Because her Aunt Mira is overweight and an outcast in the town, she must be like Colie. Because Norman has shown a romantic interest in her, he must want sex. Because Isabel is thin and gorgeous, she must not be able to understand Colie's struggles. But Colie has it all wrong. Mira cares nothing for the opinions of others, believing herself fortunate to be surrounded by her work and friends. Norman is simply a sensitive young man who sees in Colie the beauty that she cannot seem to realize is there. And Isabel was once an overweight young girl lacking in confidence and self-respect, surely capable of understanding Colie's pain. Colie must learn to see beyond the surface and give others the chance that she so often longed for. In doing so, she must take a risk and expose herself to potential heartbreak, simultaneously gaining the opportunity to experience invaluable relationships that ultimately help her figure out who she really is.

Women and Worth

Colie's development of self does not happen on its own. She is supported and guided by several key figures in her life who help her tap the potential that has always existed within her. The females who surround her, in particular, give her the push she needs to assert herself and reject the negative self-image that has plagued her for so long. These women play a contrasting role to the females who remain on the outside of this caring community and seek ways to tear her down.

The Women Within

Colie lives in a community of women whose members allow and encourage her to grow into herself. Although she believes she is alone and isolated, Colie is touched, shaped, and nurtured by three very different females—Kiki, Mira, and Isabel.

Colie feels both physically and emotionally isolated from her mother, Kiki. She misses the old days on the road, the pre-fame days, the fat days, when the two would escape to the highway when times got tough and revel in the opportunity to begin anew. Back then, it was Colie and her mom against the world. Now, it feels like Colie is alone in her fight. Despite this perceived abandonment, Kiki has not given up on her daughter. She exerts her influence across many miles. While she is away on tour, her presence persists, and her words reach her daughter when Colie least expects and most needs them.

Through various media, Kiki encourages her to believe in the possibility of change. One evening while flipping channels on the television, Colie comes across an interview with her mother on a London news program. Kiki touts a new weight-loss philosophy that is grounded in the belief that all people have the potential to change, to become, to transform themselves from caterpillars to butterflies. They simply need to believe. These words spark memories of earlier times:

> And there was that sparkle in her eye, bright enough to reach across an ocean and still get me. My mother believed, and she could make you, too. She'd believed me all the way out of forty-five-and-a-half pounds. She'd believed us from living out of the car to having anything we wanted. (98)

Now, perhaps, she will help Colie believe herself into seeing the girl she really is, a work in progress, one who has the capacity to become. During a long-distance telephone conversation, this message of change is reiterated. Colie asks Kiki if she was always as brave as she seems to be now. After reminding Colie of the sadness and uncertainty that accompanied the fat days, Kiki tells her daughter that self-confidence does not necessarily begin from within. In Kiki's case, it was not until her aerobics class participants began to look to her for strength and guidance that she began to realize how they depended upon her and how they perceived her. She claims she faked it until, somewhere along the line, what they saw became real. From Kiki's perspective, self-confidence "starts with the rest of the world, and leads back to you" (117). Colie must start seeing in herself what others have told her exists. Kiki's words reach Colie a final time through a motivational tape that Mira listens to as she falls asleep. As Colie places the headphones over her ears and closes her eyes, she is reminded once more that change is possible and desirable, though risky. Her mother's voice tells her that true failure in life results from refusing to try. Those who fail are those who "sit on the couch and whine and moan and wait for the world to change for them" (209). Our destiny is ours to decide.

Aunt Mira also plays a key role in helping Colie see the world and herself in a different light. Her lessons revolve around a repair metaphor that helps Colie realize that standardized perfection is too much to expect from anything or anyone. We cannot and should not all fit the same pattern in life. Mira surrounds herself with second-hand, often damaged, merchandise. Her home is filled with objects that need a tweak here or a wiggle there to work properly. Colie has trouble understanding Mira's unwillingness to purchase anything new that works perfectly every time. When she asks Mira about her habit, Mira tells her that perfection is an awful lot to expect from something. She adds, "If something doesn't work exactly right, or maybe needs some special treatment, you don't just throw it away. Everything can't be fully operational all the time. Sometimes we need to have the patience to give something the little nudge it needs" (118–19). Finding this little something is the key. Repairs often require one simple adjustment. Determining just what needs to be adjusted is the most difficult part. Colie must adjust her self-image and accept that which she sees. She must follow Mira's lead and realize that, though imperfect, she works in her own way.

At the start of the novel, it seems that Isabel, a waitress at the Last Chance, will be the most unlikely character to support Colie. Her first words to Colie are critical, telling her that her lip ring is repulsive. It is Isabel's candor, however, that most helps Colie find her way. Isabel tells it like it is and forces Colie to see the truth about her past and her potential future. Dessen, too, finds inspiration in Isabel's character, noting, "It's Isabel's voice I hear in my head when I'm feeling spineless."

When Caroline Dawes, a beautiful and cruel classmate, visits the restaurant, sees Colie, and assails her with insults, Isabel witnesses the event without intruding, testing Colie to see how she will respond to the attack. After Caroline departs, Isabel steps in and offers the only kind of support she knows how to give—brutal honesty. She takes Colie to her house, tells her that "the world is chock full of bitchy girls"(84), and suggests that she pluck her eyebrows and re-dye her hair. When Colie asks Isabel why she is being so nice to her, Isabel angrily tells Colie that she must expect respect and not be surprised when others treat her as they should. Isabel taps her temple and says, "Believe in yourself up here and it will make you stronger than you could ever imagine" (88). Isabel's confidence is infectious, and Colie witnesses a change in herself, however slight, when she sees her reflection in the mirror. The transformation has begun.

Isabel lends further support to Colie when she invites her to a Chick Night with Morgan and helps her prepare for the Fourth of July fireworks. As Isabel works her magic with a curl of the eyelashes here and a twist of the hair there, Colie again sees the emergence of the pretty girl she has hidden behind her ragged, black hair and sullen face. Isabel prompts Colie to stand up straight, put her shoulders back, and, most significantly, remove her lip ring, her touchstone, her security blanket. Colie is now fully exposed. When they arrive at the festivities, Isabel gives Colie an excuse to go back to the car, urging her to stand tall and show herself off due to her gorgeous appearance. Isabel's words remain with Colie as she walks among the crowd and become especially key when she finds herself face to face, once again, with Caroline Dawes. Isabel's confidence in her gives Colie the courage to break free from her conditioned reaction to hurtful words. Instead of quietly waiting out the storm, Colie faces the assault and tells Caroline to get over her hatred, to just let it go. When reflecting back on that night, Colie is proud of herself but cannot imagine having achieved what she did without Isabel. Isabel forces Colie to take responsibility for her changed self. She tells her that all she did was dye her hair and do her make-up. "It was all you," Isabel reminds Colie. "Because for once, you believed in yourself. You believed you were beautiful and so did the rest of the world" (217). Colie could do it all along.

The Women Without
Although each of the women in Colie's life shares bits of wisdom, Colie must accept the support of these women for their words to have any effect. She must see herself as they do—strong and beautiful and unique. She must believe them. No one else can defend her, and until she believes she is worth defending, neither can she. Ultimately, it is the presence of those females outside this community that rallies Colie to the cause and incites her to accept the truth about herself. Colie has withstood the snide remarks, rude jibes, and regular emotional beatings of Caroline Dawes for years. As she grows tired of allowing Caroline to ruin her life, Colie knows that she must step up to act. Armed with the support of Kiki, Mira, and Isabel, she is now ready to go into battle for herself. As she faces Caroline, she is alone but not alone. She is standing on her own, but the words of her mother and friends float in her mind and push her to do what needs to be done. On this Fourth of July, Colie asserts her independence and knows that everything has changed.

Colie's new vision of herself is developed, too, through the presence of Bea Williamson, a snotty woman in town who treats Mira like Caroline treats Colie. Bea makes fun of Mira's colorful clothing, the fact that she is a regular customer at the annual church bazaar, and the way she opens her home to stray people and animals. While witnessing Bea's behavior, Colie sees, from an outside perspective, the pettiness and cowardess that Bea and Caroline represent. Now that Colie is not the target, she has a clearer view of the attackers. No longer concerned with what is at stake for herself, she does not go into panic mode and is afforded a more realistic vision of the reality that these women represent. These women are powerful only when we allow them to be. Mira seems unaware of Bea's comments, when, in reality, she knows what Bea thinks of her and really doesn't care. As a result, Bea's antics seem foolish and juvenile; she is powerless over Mira, as Mira refuses to relinquish control over her own sense of self, a lesson Colie learns in her own encounter with Caroline.

Men and the Community of Women

Gender expectations among men play a key role in this novel. The distinction between the two kinds of men in the story is captured well in Morgan's analogy between men and mayonnaise: "Mayonnaise is a lot like men. It can make everything much better, adding flavor and ease to your life. Or, it can just be sticky and gross and make you nauseous"(49). Among the male characters in the novel, only Norman improves the lives of those around him. He least fits the classic description of the stereotypical male and lends nurturing support to those in need. The other men either fit or advocate a masculine identity and, in the end, damage those around them by trying to maintain this standard.

The Masculine Ideal

Mark could be the poster child for the all-American male. He is literally tall, dark, and handsome, is trying to make a name for himself on the baseball field, and sweeps Morgan off her feet with his smooth compliments. He is charming and manipulative, telling Morgan what she wants to hear but using her just the same. He fails to arrive during scheduled visits (or does so several hours late), refuses to give Morgan his telephone

number or itinerary after she surprises him and a stripper during an unan-
nounced visit, and refuses to discuss wedding details although he and
Morgan are officially engaged. He has excuses for his delays, affairs, and
reluctance to set a date, and manages to keep Morgan at home waiting
for him until she surprises him and the stripper, now his pregnant wife,
once again. Mark hurts the woman who truly loves him and ends up
trapped in his attempt to lead the carefree life of a swinging bachelor.

A Father and His Sons
Norman's father, Norm, Sr., wants to live out his male fantasy through
his sons. He has found success with his two eldest boys. One is a football player, and the other wins a college scholarship as a basketball star.
Norm takes pride in these boys because their choices and successes emulate his way of thinking. They are not necessarily better people than
Norman, his youngest son; they simply do what is expected and accepted. As a result, Norm has difficulty accepting the path Norman has
opted to take. He takes no pride in his son's pursuit of art as a career.
Even if Norman is no athlete, the least he could do is help with the
family used car business, Norm thinks. When Norman reveals his alternate intentions, Norm refuses to support him emotionally or financially, even though Norman has already won a scholarship to art
school. He never even bothers to view one of his son's paintings.
Norm's refusal to accept his son for who he is leads Norman to flee, taking refuge in Mira's basement. Morgan explains Norman's situation to
Colie, giving her a lesson in acceptance in the process, when she tells
her, "He'd made up his mind about what he wanted Norman to be.
He'd assumed too much. And it's so sad, that his dad just doesn't get it.
He never has" (178). This lack of understanding and an unwillingness
to alter his expectations sever Norm's relationship with his son.

Norman and the Community of Women
Norman is a long-haired, quirky artist Morgan and Isabel describe as
special. He is sensitive and compassionate, the nicest, sweetest boy the
two waitresses have ever met. But Norman is not a coward. Rather than
live under the expectations of his father, he, at seventeen, packs up his
bags and leaves home. He would rather live by the dumpsters behind
the restaurant than under the roof of a man who refuses to accept him.

Norman bases his principles on common decency, respect, and personal pride rather than a socially determined and ordained view of what he is supposed to be as a man. He chooses to act in accordance with what he believes is right rather than what others profess as correct.

It takes time for Colie to see this truth about Norman. Although the women around her see Norman as both bold and kind, her view remains limited. To her, at least initially, he is simply a hippie art freak who collects naked mannequins and sunglasses, works as a cook in the restaurant, listens to dead head music, and probably does drugs. Although Norman is nothing but nice to her—helping her learn the ropes as a waitress, giving her a pair of sunglasses as a gift from the heart, and asking her to sit for a portrait—Colie does not appreciate him or realize just how wonderful he is until she learns the truth of his past and moves beyond her assumptions to get to know the boy that the women around her adore. She comes to realize her error: "All I knew about him was what I'd seen and assumed. So many times I'd sat watching from my room as he lugged strange objects into his apartment. . . . Then there were the portraits. That slow, loping way of moving. The sunglasses" (176–77). Colie learns to trust Norman and reveals to him the secrets of her past that have trapped her in a limited view of self.

Norman becomes yet another source of support in the development of Colie's sense of self. He has believed in her all along. He not only sees her as beautiful but helps her to see herself as such when he reveals the portrait he has painted of her. When she glimpses the girl on the canvas, Colie cannot believe it is her. The girl who stares back at her is beautiful, "not in the cookie-cutter way" of magazine models or "in the easy, almost effortless style of a girl like Caroline Dawes." The girl who stares back knows "she is not like the others" and is fine with that (221). When Colie asks Norman if that is how he sees her, he tells her that that is how she is. Norman allows himself to see the world from an unbiased perspective. He need not be one of the guys and can function within the community of women. Near the end of the novel, Morgan, Isabel, and Colie dance. This is what girls do, they say, when they have no other recourse. Frank, Isabel's current beau, flees the scene, feeling awkward and uncomfortable in this setting. In contrast, Norman dances with the women, joining their circle and their community, forging his own identity without regard for social norms.

The Charm of the Eccentric

The primary source of humor in *Keeping the Moon* resides in the quirkiness of the characters who live life according to their own rules. Mira, the queen of eccentricity, takes center stage in this arena, showing us the grace and insight that comes with being just a little off-center. She avidly watches professional wrestling, keeping track of the stories that take place out of the ring, wondering, for example, "why El Gigantico cares about Lola anyway, she's just as trashy as she can be" (17). She visits the grocery store and buys nothing but various breakfast cereals. She is seen regularly riding her bicycle into town, Terminator glasses in place, red hair flying, purple high-tops pedaling furiously. She even boasts a unique career. Although she has made her fortune in the creation of NonniCards, greeting cards that feature a little girl in a sailor suit and her mother's high-heeled shoes, Mira wants another challenge. She thus turns to the creation of death cards for every death imaginable—dead mailmen, dead bosses, dead co-workers, even dead hamsters. One card reads, "There comes a time when we must accept the loss of someone who may not have been truly real but was very real in our hearts" (213)—a condolence for a dead soap opera character. Mira is her own person. Instead of mocking her, we find ourselves chuckling at her uniqueness and reveling in her willingness to live life on her terms.

Not everyone in town appreciates Mira's ways, however. When she first arrives, she offers to teach a community center art class formerly taught by a woman who would allow participants to paint only flowers and animals. In typical Mira fashion, she encourages her students to venture beyond this limited perspective and explore the human form and avant garde methods. She invites the mailman, seventy-year-old Mr. Rooter, to model for the class—in the nude. Although Mira does not understand what all the fuss is about, many in the community begin to distance themselves from her (and those enrolled in the art class go back to painting flowers and animals). This separation is heightened when Mira fights against the removal of controversial books from the middle school library. Morgan tells Colie that Mira makes others nervous.

Colie learns slowly to appreciate Mira despite the fact that her unorthodox ways cause her to be embarrassed at first. As noted earlier, Mira saves everything, both literally and figuratively. Her house is filled with remnants of her past as well as half-working items recovered from second-hand sources. To remind herself and those with whom she lives how to function amid these not-quite-right household items, she covers her home with reminder notes: STICKS ON THE LEFT SIDE; BURNS THINGS FAST; CONSISTENTLY FIVE MINUTES BEHIND; JIGGLE TO GET 11. Although Colie finds this behavior bizarre, she begins to see Mira's logic, realizing that Mira uses all of these things despite their imperfect condition. For Mira, "there were no lost causes. Everything, and everyone, had its purpose" (119). Mira serves to make us smile and help Colie realize that the typical way is not always the best way.

Morgan and Isabel, too, lend humor to the story through the volatile and loyal nature of their friendship. Modeled after the waitresses with whom Dessen worked and representative of the humor, dedication, and emotion they possessed, the two young women could not be any more different from one another. Morgan is a tall, bony girl with big feet and postures and expressions that remind Colie of a dodo bird, while Isabel is curvy, blonde, and gorgeous. Yet, the bond they share is solid and enviable; they know one another well. They play off one another like a comedy duo unaware of just how funny they are together. When Morgan threatens to quit her waitressing job for the third time in two weeks, tearing off her apron and heading outside to confront the patrons who left her too little a tip, Isabel casually waits for her return, knowing that Morgan will return claiming that the guilty party just left and retying her apron. When Mark comes for one of his one-night visits and leaves before making any wedding plans, Isabel warns Colie about the devilled eggs that are sure to accompany Morgan to work that day. Her comfort food, Morgan is notorious for making the treats when she is upset. Colie can't help but laugh when Morgan arrives, eggs in hand. When Isabel confronts Morgan about Mark and his earlier escapades, questioning why Morgan still has feelings for him, Isabel claims that he is not even a talented baseball player. Morgan defends him, claiming, "He doesn't even lead the team in errors anymore!" (139). Although the inclusion of this friendship provides more than simply laughable moments, the comedic element therein shows Colie (and us) that strong relationships are grounded in the ability to laugh at ourselves and those closest to us.

Some may argue that the presence of two grown women as significant characters might lessen the novel's teen appeal and call into question its classification as a young adult text. Indeed, Morgan and Isabel are no longer high school students under the auspices of parents or guardians. They support themselves financially and deal with typically adult concerns such as marriage. In many ways, however, they are representative of the big sisters we might wish for ourselves, young women not too much older than us who serve as guides in the maturation process. We look to them for guidance on how to behave with boys, wear our make-up, and assert ourselves as young women, too. They are there should we need a shoulder for our tears, an ear for our woes, or a footprint to follow as we maneuver our way through adolescence. They are admirable models of women who have survived the process and emerged able and willing to share lessons learned.

The Author's Craft

In this novel, more so than in those discussed thus far, Dessen illustrates her ability to craft a powerful, coherent story. She weaves several images and motifs through the text that serve to heighten the themes she explores.

The Butterfly

Dessen uses the image of the caterpillar transforming into a butterfly to trace Colie's progression from a girl lacking in confidence to a young woman on the way to figuring out who she is. With its origins in Kiki's new weight-loss philosophy, the metaphor requires that the caterpillars do more than watch the butterflies. They, themselves, must become. At the outset, Colie has shed her cocoon, losing the weight that padded her for so long, but has not yet found the ability to transform herself. At this point, all she can do is "stand on the ground and look up at the sky, not quite ready yet to leap and rise" (99). This fear of taking off is embodied in Colie's hesitation to dance in front of others. As a result of her humiliating experience at her first middle school dance, she prefers to stay low, belly scraping the floor, watching rather than dancing like the "lightest and brightest of butterflies" (129). It is not until she sees herself in Norman's painting, realizing that that girl would not be afraid to dance, that she allows herself to soar.

The Moon

The mystery of a lunar eclipse symbolizes Colie's development as she learns to accept that life is not always predictable or in our control. Sometimes we just have to have faith that all will be well if we just let go. Mira, the amateur astrologer, is thrilled to learn that a full lunar eclipse will soon arrive. The "cosmos is getting ready to *freak* out. Big changes coming" (190), she tells Colie. Norman, too, anticipates the event due to a childhood memory of his first eclipse. He remembers being a six-year-old boy camped out in his backyard with his two older brothers anxiously waiting for the moon to disappear. Once it did, he feared it would never return, that some entity was keeping the moon. He wanted to believe the moon would never go away, but, in the moment, he was not certain that this was true. He tells Colie:

> It's strange when you've always been told something is true, like the moon *will* come back. You need proof. And while you wait, you feel the entire balance of your world just tipping. It's crazy. But when it's over, and it *does* come back, that's the best, because it's all you want, everything narrows to just *that*. (193)

Although Colie has been told by her mother, Mira, Isabel, and Norman that she is indeed beautiful, she still feels as though she needs proof. She learns, however, that, although it is hard, she must, "believe in what [she] can't fully understand" (228) and accept on faith that she is all they claim her to be. She must let go of her hurtful past and realize that she has known the truth about herself all along, even if her enemies have not.

The Music

This novel has the potential to have a compelling soundtrack. Woven throughout are snippets of song that remind us of the power of music to serve as both a reflection of and influence upon that which we are feeling. It has the power to hold us back and free us. When Colie feels most lost and alone, she turns to her music—music that screams and thunders and hates as much as she wants to—for solace. Her artists of choice play songs like "Bite" that involve yelling as loudly as possible over the blaring drums. This music not only represents her negative emotional state but reinforces her anger and frustration, thus perpetuating her initial emotions.

In stark contrast, Isabel and Morgan not only see themselves in the music they play but allow that music to change them. They have a CD collection that would be the envy of any music lover, and their titles of choice range from the oldies to Top Forty to disco. Their lives are set to music. When Isabel is sad, she puts on Led Zeppelin, which Morgan hates. When Morgan misses Mark, she plays Celine Dion, which Isabel despises. The friends refuse to allow one another to become mired in the music representative of their current state. They have worked out a system in which they take turns selecting their music choices. Zeppelin and Dion both get limited play, and the associated feelings are recognized and moved beyond.

Isabel and Morgan have discovered the role that music plays in their friendship. It can serve to communicate what neither young woman could say with words. When Isabel tells Morgan how she really feels about Mark and urges Morgan to accept the truth about him, the discussion turns into a full-blown argument, complete with yelling, insults, and slamming doors. While Colie comforts Morgan behind the locked door of the bathroom, the two suddenly hear the opening lyrics, "At first I was afraid, I was petrified." These words serve as an apology by Isabel, a peace offering, an invitation to join her in a dance. Morgan smiles at her reflection in the mirror, wipes her eyes, opens the door, and joins her friend. Music has the power to reunite.

Colie witnesses these events and is changed by them. At first, she loves to sit on the roof outside her window and listen to the evening musical choices of Isabel and Morgan, keeping her distance but learning nevertheless. Soon, she even begins to appreciate Norman's hippie music. In the end, she is inspired to dance, to allow music to aid in the healing process. When Morgan is devastated by Mark's betrayal, she is inconsolable. She eventually tires of crying and turns to music, blaring those same words, "At first I was afraid, I was petrified," and claiming that there is nothing more she can do on this night but dance. When she invites Colie to join her, Colie allows Morgan to pull her into the music, to lose herself in song, not as a means to justify her anger but to heal and move forward.

Keeping the Moon is a story of metamorphosis, one that encourages readers to look beyond the past and have faith in one's self and the future. Although Dessen hesitates to name a favorite among her books, she identifies this novel as a serious contender. When she is "feeling particularly wimpy,"[3] she says, she thinks of this story and finds in herself the courage to believe in her potential.

Notes

1. Sarah Dessen, *"Keeping the Moon," Personal Website*, at www.sarahdessen.com/keeping.html (accessed 4 March 2003).

2. Review of *Keeping the Moon*, by Sarah Dessen, *Kirkus Reviews*, 15 August 1999, 1309–10.

3. Dessen. *"Keeping the Moon," Personal Website*.

CHAPTER SIX

~

Escaping Submersion and Submission in the Nightmare of *Dreamland*

"Dreams, and plans, and a stark desire to change your life, all on your own. I wanted that too" (237). Dessen's fourth novel, *Dreamland*, explores the difficulties inherent in learning to love ourselves. In order to fully accept ourselves as we are and as we wish to be, we must respect ourselves enough to defend our own honor, take risks, and break free from the bindings, both self- and other-imposed, that restrain us. For Dessen, the novel is about "suddenly having to find your way when someone has always led the way for you before."[1] It is about finding the strength to trust in what we know to be right and summoning the courage to follow our own lead.

In writing the novel, which stands unique in tone and weightiness of topic from that of her other works, Dessen was forced to trust herself and allow her words to go "deeper," to a place that, as a writer, was "really challenging."[2] The story of Caitlin and Rogerson originally played out in one of Dessen's unpublished novels. While reading a book on Christmas Day of 1997, however, Dessen found herself moved by the use of the word "dreamland" in a simple sentence. She imagined a mother standing silhouetted in the doorway of a darkened bedroom, promising to meet her child in this magical place of sleep. Caitlin and Rogerson were resurrected, and a new novel with additional characters, subplots, and themes resulted. The process was slow-going, and, in the writing of some scenes, Dessen had to leave the room, close her eyes, and compose herself before continuing. She notes, "It's hard to create a character, like Caitlin, on the page and then systematically break her down to nothing before you can begin to build her up again."[3]

Dessen's courage and willingness to follow her own lead have been rewarded. Critics have identified the novel as "another perfect pitch offering"[4] that "goes far beyond the teen problem novel in a story rich with symbolism, dark scenes of paralyzing dread, quirky and memorable characters, and gleams of humor."[5] An American Library Association Best Book for Young Adults and Popular Paperback for Young Adults, an Amazon.com Editors Choice for 2000, and a 2001 and 2002 New York Library Book for the Teen Age, the novel offers "compelling reading with contemporary teen appeal."[6] The book is both exhausting and uplifting in its treatment of Caitlin, the primary protagonist, and her struggles to find herself.

On the day of her sixteenth birthday, Caitlin's seemingly perfect older sister, Cass, runs away from home. Left to deal with the aftermath of such a loss, Caitlin struggles to find her way out of the shadow of her sister, whose presence remains despite her absence. Feeling inadequate and unable to take her sibling's place, Caitlin strikes out to forge an identity of her own. She is drawn to Rogerson Biscoe, an enticing and dangerous young man who, with his dreadlocks and criminal record, is like no boy Cass would have ever dated. Caitlin is intrigued by the experiences he provides her. Nights with him are spent supplying drugs to various customers rather than double-dating at the drive-in or mini golf course. Caitlin finds herself emotionally committed to Rogerson when she witnesses his father's abusive anger and Rogerson's subsequent pain and hurt. Soon, however, she becomes the punching bag for Rogerson in a depressing (and powerfully realistic) cycle of domestic violence. Although Caitlin is surrounded by family members and friends who care about her deeply, she alone must summon the strength necessary to end her own downward spiral.

Forging Our Own Way

The struggle for self-autonomy experienced by several key characters in the novel reveals that when we become mired in the expectations of others, we experience a perceived and/or real lack of control over our lives. Others become authorities on our lives, shaping our existence in a way that may not suit our desires or needs. "It's so easy to get caught up in what people expect of you. Sometimes, you can just lose yourself" (20). Three young women, Corinna, Cass, and Caitlin, experience this loss of self under the influence of external forces that constrict their growing desire for independence. In order to break free from these bonds and escape the accompanying sense of helplessness, the women must reassert control over their lives, resume the decision-making process, and rekindle the passion for living on their own terms.

Fleeing to Freedom
Corinna is the chain-smoking, bangle-wearing, TV-watching young waitress who befriends Caitlin when she accompanies Rogerson on a drug delivery to the run-down farmhouse she shares with her lover, Dave. She and Dave have dated since high school and live together despite her parents' disapproval. Corinna no longer speaks with her family, claiming her mother and father hated Dave on sight because he interfered with their plans for her—chastity, college, and a career in law. She tells Caitlin angrily, "They'd already, like, decided exactly what I was supposed to do, and be" (123). Although she does not regret her choices in life, Corinna feels as though she has failed her parents by not fulfilling all that they had planned for her. She is courageous in her decision to leave but remains under the control of her parents when she allows their disappointed faces and critical comments to influence her sense of self.

Corinna is a romantic who loves happy endings. She watches repeatedly the infomercial that features before and after shots of the young acne sufferer who tries a new medication with great success, and she dreams of traveling to California where the days are always sunny and movie stars dine alongside everyday residents in local cafes. She believes in the power of love and, though poor financially, remains with Dave (who spends his days sleeping in the next room). In choosing to remain with the unemployed, often stoned man in her life who has no desire to go to California, she has moved from one set of expectations to another. Her parents wanted everything from her, while Dave wants her to do nothing. In order to make her own dreams come true, Corinna must abandon her holding pattern and take flight. She can still be a romantic and venture to the land of her dreams, but, in order to do so, she must summon the pragmatism she demonstrated when she left home to be with Dave, this time to leave Dave. Her escape allows her to soar unencumbered.

Avoiding the Trap

Cass lives under the watchful eye of her over-involved mother—a PTA volunteer, Junior Leaguer, and school chaperone who knows by heart her daughter's daily schedule, SAT scores, sports team stats, and GPA. Cass is the girl who is elected student body president two years running, scores the winning goal, volunteers at the local soup kitchen, and is accepted to Yale. She is the girl whom others admire and wish to emulate; her happiness is assumed. But Cass is also the girl who realizes that motives are just as important as actions. She questions why she follows this path of seeming perfection, living according to expectations that are not of her own creation and allowing others to make the choices that determine her fate. As she faces a college experience at Yale, she goes through the motions, smiling and accepting the congratulations of others and dreading the continuation of life under rules with which she would rather not comply. In an attempt to resume control over her present and future, she flees, traveling to New York to live with her new boyfriend, Adam, and begin again. In a letter to Caitlin, she explains her choice:

> It was a relief to know when I walked out that door that I was letting everyone down. I'd spent so much of my life working hard to make Mom and Dad happy, to be what everyone thought I should be. Coming here was like starting from scratch, and scary as it is sometimes, I like it. . . . Up here, away from everyone's notions, I can be whatever I want. (238–39)

Like Corinna, Cass responds to impending entrapment by striking out on her own, taking back the life that has been subsumed by the wishes of others. She will now determine what is best for her.

Finding Her Way

Unlike Corinna and Cass, Caitlin does not at first feel the need to comply with others' expectations. Cass has always taken center-stage, and

Caitlin, although envious of her sister, is willing to take a back seat. Caitlin imagines Cass' life as golden, filled with repeated successes and ever-present parental pride. She admires Cass' dresser mirror, surrounded by ribbons, awards, and photos of friends, very unlike her own mirror that contains only a photo of her best friend, a third-place ribbon from horseback riding, and a B honor roll certificate. Although Caitlin envies her sister, she also loves her, finding in her her greatest source of support. She has always assumed that Cass would be there to lead the way. Now that she is gone, Caitlin must forge ahead on her own, unable to depend upon her sister to fulfill the expectations that she herself feels she cannot.

Caitlin attempts to venture down her own path when she tries out and earns a spot on the cheerleading squad, something Cass avoided due to her own interest in athletics rather than short skirts and cartwheels. Ironically, Caitlin finds herself in the same situation as her sister when her mother becomes obsessively involved in her cheerleading life, posting her schedule on the refrigerator, serving as a cheer parent, and attending every game. As her own life becomes less and less her own, Caitlin wonders if Cass' life was really so ideal.

Caitlin finds her unique path when she begins to date Rogerson, the bad boy whom her parents would surely forbid her to see if they knew the truth about him and his criminal record. He gives Caitlin exactly what she desires—a secret life beyond the control of her increasingly invasive mother. As Caitlin heads out the door for her first date with Rogerson, she takes ownership of her actions, claiming, "I wanted this to be all mine, not part of any schedule or plan she could claim as her own" (73). Rogerson gives her, too, just what she needs to come out from under Cass' shadow, to create her own life story. This story, however, is one of sadness and fear, as her life becomes "less something she participates in than something that washes over her."[7] The fact that she is with a boy who beats her reinforces her belief that she is weaker than Cass. What Caitlin most loves about Rogerson at the start of their relationship is the fact that he takes her far from anywhere that Cass had been. Now that he is hitting her, she is even more removed from her sister who, she claims, would never have remained in such a relationship. She has finally overshadowed her sister, exceeding even her own expectations, but not in the way that she had hoped.

With the help of Dr. Marshall, a psychologist at the treatment center to which she is admitted after the abuse is discovered, Caitlin eventually recognizes the self-imposed expectations that she has placed upon herself out of a desire to keep from letting her sister down. The symbolic import of the scar across Caitlin's temple weighs heavy. The result of a childhood sandbox incident involving a wayward shovel, the scar represents the imperfection Caitlin feels when compared with her seemingly perfect sister. She is flawed and will never measure up. Her greatest fear is imagining what her sister must think of her now that the truth of her weakness has been revealed. She tells Dr. Marshall, "It's just that I've always been the weaker one, the less talented. The perennial second-place also-ran. The more likely to screw up. And now, with this, I've, like, totally proved it" (236). Dr. Marshall urges Caitlin to accept that Cass, too, knows pain. She is imperfect. Perfect people do not run away from home with no explanation, leaving family members behind to pick up the pieces and replace the void. Caitlin has the right to be angry with Cass, to let her down from the pedestal upon which she has been perched for years, and to stand beside her as an equal. Caitlin learns the truth of this when Cass shares her own envy toward and dependence upon her younger sister, telling her that Caitlin is the one she thinks of when she is at her weakest, that Caitlin is the one who pulls her through the difficult times. These words help Caitlin understand that perception and reality are not always the same and that we sometimes wrongfully expect too much of others and ourselves.

The Dreamland Metaphor

Drawing upon symbolism from T. S. Eliot's poem "The Love Song of J. Alfred Prufrock," Dessen explores Caitlin's search for self through the metaphor of dreamland, a place that offers ironically more nightmares than respite. She first likens Caitlin to the speaker in the poem who, when refused a song by the mermaids, expresses a "separateness from the rest of the world, the kind of dream-state he is in, all by himself. He says he's underwater, with these mermaids who both accept and reject him" (163). Caitlin is ultimately unlike the speaker, however, in that she is capable of action and human interaction and refuses to retreat into a world of fantasy. For Prufrock, "it is the human element—the real world—that ultimately does him in, as seen in the last line . . . *Till human voices wake us, and we drown*" (163). For Caitlin, it is the human element, the voices of those around her, that saves her from drowning and helps her return to shore.

Once Cass leaves, Caitlin feels as though she is going through the motions, floating along, waiting for something to happen. Her parents are consumed by sadness and confusion over Cass' departure, and Caitlin is at a loss as to how to proceed without her older sister's guidance. Her wake-up call comes in the form of Rogerson, who offers excitement and diversion, uncharted territory for her to explore. Rogerson knows nothing of her life at home, her sister, or her parents, as he attends a different school and runs with a different crowd. Caitlin, then, can be anything or anyone with him that she desires to be. With Rogerson, Caitlin feels like she is making her own choices, "living awake after being in a dreamworld for so long" (94). Life is fast-paced; she is always in transit, enjoying the constant movement and sense of the unknown around the next bend.

This constant movement becomes paralyzing, however, after the abuse begins. Caitlin feels lost and alone as she carries the burden of her secret. She hides "the bruises and retreats into numb isolation, feeling trapped but lacking the will to escape."[8] At one point, she claims, "it had been exciting, new, to always be in transit. But now I felt like I was drifting, sucked down by an undertow, and too far out to swim back to the shore" (167). Her teachers, family, and friends notice the change in her and reach out to pull her back, but, for Caitlin, this dreamland is preferable. She wants only to ignore the human voices as they call her name again and again, "pulling [her] upward into light, to drown" (168). For now, it is easier to remain a victim of Rogerson's wrath than to admit the truth and be judged as weak.

Once Caitlin is beaten, literally and figuratively, on the front lawn of her parents' house, she no longer has the energy to hide the truth. Although she cannot extricate herself on her own, she gives in to the voices and is freed from the depths. She hears the voices shaking her awake and allows them to pull her to the surface. To this point, she "had kept silent, drowning, by choice" (242). With time, therapy, support, and the absence of Rogerson, Caitlin makes progress. She feels herself swimming harder, getting closer and closer to the surface, until she fully accepts her story as her own, both good and bad, and breaks through to finally breathe on her own.

Exploring a Problem in a Novel

The complexity of *Dreamland* makes it more than a simple problem book. Dessen is grateful, in fact, that the novel has not been labeled an "issue book," implying that she set out to write a story about domestic violence. Indeed there is so much more in the novel. Yet, the fact that Dessen does explore the realities of such an experience gives readers a glimpse into the world of abuse that is frightening and educational. This is essential given the fact that one out of every five teenage girls in America will fall victim to such a situation, and one third to one half of married women will be beaten by their spouses.[9] The novel takes on heavy issues without pulling any punches. We watch as Caitlin tries to stay afloat amidst flailing fists and harsh words, "caught in a trap that is baited with love and need."[10] Dessen "writes with utter realism as she describes Caitlin's descent, first into drugs, then into sex, and finally into a relationship that becomes violent."[11] It is this honesty that makes Caitlin's tragedy so poignant and educative.

The Solace of Sex and Drugs

Before Rogerson begins to hit her, Caitlin is willing to take risks but recognizes the morality (or immorality) of her choices. Sexually, Caitlin moves much more quickly with Rogerson than she has with any other boy. Although inexperienced, she is ready to forge her own way, a non-Cass way. On the first night she and Rogerson meet, she spends several hours making out with him in his car. As she leaves the car, buttoning her shirt and sticking her bra in the pocket of her cheerleading outfit, she notes how quickly and how far she has fallen. Yet, when it comes to issues of intercourse, Caitlin wants to take her time. She does not want it to happen "in some mad rush or on a random Tuesday afternoon" (109). Her drug use prior to the abuse, too, is presented as innocent experimentation as she tries on her new identity. One afternoon at Corinna's, the choice to smoke pot "just seemed *right*, or as right as anything technically wrong could be" (118). At this point, she retains an awareness of her choices and some semblance of control over them.

Caitlin's autonomy dissipates, however, once Rogerson strikes her. She now struggles to stay afloat, making decisions grounded in nothing more than a desire to survive from one day to the next. Sex and drugs no longer provide excitement and an opportunity for rebellion but solace and escape from the reality that she refuses to acknowledge. On Christmas Eve, Caitlin sleeps with Rogerson. She relates the event in the most unemotional, matter of fact, way, noting simply, "That night, I slept with him for the first time" (165). From then on, she tries to convince herself that sexual contact brings them closer together, not only physically but emotionally. She wants to be able to trust Rogerson, to believe that her decision to remain with him is justified. It is difficult, then, for Caitlin to reconcile the two Rogersons in her mind—the boy who caresses her gently and holds her closely after sex cannot be the same boy who hits her. The drugs provide both distance and relief from Caitlin's confusion and pain. Although Dessen was concerned that her treatment of this issue might make it seem "frivolous," even "attractive,"[12] the drug use is not painted in a positive light. It reinforces, instead, Rogerson's power over Caitlin as well as her willingness to accept his domination. When Caitlin is stoned, her problems seem to fade away, at least for a time. She hates feeling out of control and out of touch but sees this as more desirable than the alternative of real life.

The Realities of Abuse
Although Dessen says that she did no formal research into domestic abuse before writing the novel, she presents realistically the cycle of violence, denial, and hope that Caitlin experiences. When Rogerson hits Caitlin for the first time, neither she nor the reader see it coming. Dessen "doesn't telegraph Rogerson's ultimate abuse. Readers will be as blindsided by the first punch as Caitlin is."[13] Caitlin wonders if it really happened (as do we), believing it to be perhaps a dream. Rogerson says nothing about his actions, driving instead to McDonald's for a milkshake, Caitlin's favorite, telling her for the first time that he loves her, and caressing her gently and repeatedly. In hindsight, Caitlin realizes she could have left his car that night and never returned. She realizes, however, that she loves him and, perhaps more importantly, loves the girl she is when she is with him. When he kisses her goodnight, the pain subsides to nothing more than a pinprick. It is easy to pretend that

nothing happened, thus maintaining her new identity and not having to admit that she may have made a mistake.

As the abuse continues, Caitlin develops several coping mechanisms. In the midst of an attack, she takes her mind off the present by reciting bits of trivia, relying upon "the solidness and safety of facts" to see her through (156). When friends and family members ask about her bruises and bumps, she becomes a master of excuses, blaming stray elbows and slippery ice. To hide the physical evidence, she takes to wearing long- sleeved shirts and pants. She views the abuse as a sort of sports match in which injuries range from blocking bruises to hard fouls to full contact. There are rules of play that she must learn; talking with others yields a technical foul, while being late results in illegal movement. When she knows she is sure to incur Rogerson's wrath, she figures out her game plan, "working [her] defense, figuring the play, setting the pick and the run and the shoot" (213).

Despite his treatment of her, Caitlin wants to believe that Rogerson is a good person (or why would she remain with him?). Although Rogerson never says he is sorry, Caitlin accepts his gifts and gentle gestures as tokens of his remorse. She anxiously awaits the twenty-four-hour period following any attack, knowing that, for a time, she will be safe but knowing, too, that another punch or slap will follow soon enough. She searches the photographs she has taken of him, striving to find proof that he is not the monster that he is. Even when the truth is discovered, Caitlin does not want to lose Rogerson. Although he has taken everything from her, she sees him as all she has. As the police lead him away, she pulls away from her loved ones, "sobbing, screaming, everything hurting, to try and make him stay" (218). Indeed, it is only when Rogerson beats her in public that the abuse is revealed. Caitlin doesn't find her way out alone, a decision that Dessen stands by in her attempt to portray honestly the complexity of the abusive situation: "In the movies, and on TV of course, the heroine finally gets up the courage in that moment to fight back, and that's what makes the big payoff, the moment the audience claps and cheers. . . . But sometimes it just doesn't happen that way."[14]

The Labors of Recovery
In terms of Caitlin's recovery, Dessen does not offer an easy out. It is not enough that the hitting has ended and her secret has been revealed.

It is only by taking a long, hard look at herself that Caitlin is able to "work her way back to normalcy."[15] Although she desperately wants someone to rescue her, she, alone, has the power to save herself. Caitlin's experiences at Evergreen Care Center allow her to begin the process of healing. She spends time talking with Dr. Marshall and learns that misplaced blame will not help her move forward. Her mother, caught up in the loss of Cass, should perhaps have seen the changes in her daughter, and Cass should not have abandoned her family in the first place, but it is too easy to look back now and identify what could have been done better. Caitlin slowly learns not to blame herself but has difficulty putting the blame on Rogerson where she knows it belongs. She continues to miss him despite all that he put her through. In order to let go of him, she must accept the fact that she loved him. Although she has suffered, the experience with him has shaped who she is now. There is no sense in focusing on the "if onlys," as any change would mean missing something that came later—her friendship with Corinna, her discovery of photography, her opportunity to find herself. "I needed it all, in the end," she claims, "to make my own story find its finish" (242).

Women Standing Together

Dessen's women, once again, unite behind the protagonist, forming a nurturing and supportive community that Caitlin can depend upon even while experiencing her greatest personal pain. Although Caitlin's mother is concerned about Cass, she cares about Caitlin and reaches out to her on several occasions. She becomes actively—if not overly—involved in Caitlin's cheerleading experience, is hesitant to let her date Rogerson in the first place, notices the fact that her daughter's dressing habits have changed, and encourages her to spend more time with her friends rather than Rogerson. Caitlin's best friend, Rina, expresses her sadness over the fact that the two girls spend much less time together. She even goes so far as to "kidnap" Caitlin to take her to their old stomping grounds for a day of girl fun. Boo, Caitlin's free-spirited neighbor, offers quiet support, noticing a change in Caitlin and offering an ear or a shoulder without prodding or pushing. Although Caitlin, out of shame and fear, refuses to confide in these women, when she is ready, they are there to support her. Caitlin's mother organizes a visitation schedule for the time she spends in the care center, Rina provides her a connection to the world outside through her racy gossip, and Boo brings Caitlin her camera so she can begin to develop a new lens on the world.

Men and Their Emotions

The men in the novel can be judged according to the level at which they are aware and accepting of their emotions. Those who are more in touch with who they are are portrayed as more admirable.

Sensitive

Matthew and Stewart stand together at one end the spectrum. They know who they are and are willing to express their feelings. They not only experience the full range of human emotions—joy and love, confusion and deference, fear and pain—but are not afraid of appearing weak or dependent upon the support of others to see them through. Matthew, Caitlin's photography instructor, is young, energetic, and compassionate, often placing a gentle hand on Caitlin's shoulder or back to create a personal connection. He notices Caitlin's talent with a camera and takes the time to compliment her on her skill. Demonstrating great sensitivity and concern, he notes particularly how she, in a photo taken of Rogerson, has captured more than her subject wishes for her to know. When he takes her hands in his own red mittens and wishes her a Merry Christmas after class one evening, Caitlin feels safe with him, safer than she has for quite some time. His sweet and gentle disposition and willingness to reach out give Caitlin the nurturing and security she craves.

Stewart, Caitlin's neighbor and Boo's husband, is a quiet, mild-mannered art teacher at the university. With his messy, paint-flecked hair, he reminds Caitlin of a mad scientist. He believes in coed massage, winces when insects are caught in the neighbor's bug zapper outside, knows nothing of sports, and prides himself on being in touch with his emotions. When he rides his bicycle into the clothesline hanging across the yard, he blames himself and allows the line to hang intact, claiming, "It's not the fault of the clothesline. . . . It's about me respecting it as an obstacle" (19). He is physical in his affection, hugging Rogerson upon first meeting him and offering Caitlin his congratulations and a hug at the conclusion of a school awards assembly. Caitlin imagines often how ideal it would be to have him as a parent, to be able to share openly her fears and frustrations and know that she will be accepted regardless of her choices.

Distant
Caitlin's biological father, Jack, differs considerably from both Matthew and Stewart but retains our respect and admiration. Unlike Stewart, in particular, he chooses to use the bug zapper, follows the university sports teams, prides himself on being stoic, and avoids scenes of physical contact and intimacy. As the dean of students at the local university, Jack is used to handling stressful situations. According to Caitlin, he is always formal, able to distance himself from a problem, living for "*supposedlys* and *theoreticallys,* not believing anything without proper proof" (4). With Cass' departure, Jack finds himself in uncomfortable territory; this is personal. He misses Cass but shows his loss in a more subtle way. He saves every letter received from Yale, neatly stacked and unopened in a drawer in his desk. When Cass calls, however, he remains distant, talking only when prompted and commenting on the weather.

Jack is not beyond reach, however, and it is through Caitlin's pain that he learns to face the emotions he has hidden so effectively for so long. After she is admitted to the care center, he visits regularly. To get past the awkwardness and fear of having nothing about which to talk during the first visit, he impulsively purchases and brings a book, *100 Fun Card Games.* Caitlin recognizes how helpless he must feel. He has made arrangements for her stay, dealt with the insurance company, and explained to the district attorney that she will not be able to testify. She says, "He was the ultimate facilitator, but this emotional thing, with the two of us one-on-one was new to him" (231). The cards provide a common ground, a comfortable place from which a deeper relationship might develop. Sometimes while they are playing, Caitlin looks up and finds him watching her with such sadness. Remorseful of his earlier inhibitions, Jack is slowly allowing himself to let down his guard.

Uncontrollable

Rogerson is a smart underachiever who lives in the pool house owned by his wealthy parents. He has been in trouble with the law but continues his habit of supplying pot to locals. Consistent with the profile of the abuser, he is obsessive with order and time. His bedroom is spotless, and nothing angers him more than when someone is late. He divides the world into black or white; "people were either cool or assholes, situations good or bad" (93). In trying to control an uncontrollable world, he has difficulty dealing with his emotions. When confronted with inconsistencies or situations that are not easily categorized, he buries his frustrations. Unable to contain himself and these emotions, he lashes out as a result of the slightest provocation. Never saying sorry for the abuse he showers on Caitlin, he instead blames her for his attacks, attempting to attach a rationality to his irrational behavior. He tells her, "This isn't my fault. It isn't, Caitlin. You know what you did" (156).

Although Rogerson could quite readily serve as the easy target, the supreme bad guy in the story, Dessen avoids portraying him as inhuman and beyond compassion. Although he is "definitely the villain here, the author gives readers reason to spare a dash (a very small dash) of sympathy for him, too."[16] Although we cannot excuse Rogerson for his choices, we can remember that he is a product of his experiences, particularly his familial upbringing. He is known not as "the standout point guard" but as the "other son," the one who is repeating his senior year of high school and having to perform community service in lieu of serving jail time (70). His mother, a well-known realtor, is all but absent, and his father is abusive himself. When Rogerson does not arrive on time for a family gathering, his father confronts him in private, hitting Rogerson hard across the temple and reprimanding him for his irresponsible behavior. Although Caitlin, hidden in the bathroom, witnesses this exchange for the first time, it is not an isolated event. The pattern continues, and Rogerson arrives regularly at Caitlin's home with bruises on his face, unwilling to talk about what happened. There are times when Rogerson seems shocked by his actions toward Caitlin. After a bout of hitting, punching, or slapping, he looks at Caitlin in disbelief, like he cannot imagine having done what he has done. In these instances, Caitlin feels sorry for him and wonders if he is remembering his father and the "marks he'd left behind" (189). Rogerson is cruel, and his behavior is unforgivable. But with skill and realism, Dessen allows us to more fully evaluate his motives and see him as both victim and monster. His lashing out is not only the result of misplaced anger and a desire for control. It is also a product of his fear.

Humor and Hope

This novel is the darkest of Dessen's works. It is also surprisingly humorous. The mark of a truly gifted author resides in her ability to harness humor in the most unexpected, perhaps darkest, realms of where we live. In dealing with such a heavy story, Desson claims she relies on humor "to lighten the tone here and there,"[17] thus allowing us as readers to come up for air before we plunge once again into the depths of Caitlin's experience. Without trivializing or lessening the severity of Caitlin's situation, Dessen includes glimmers of humor that provide distraction and perhaps hope.

Readers are given a chance to chuckle when Dessen describes Caitlin's mother's reaction to Cass' departure. Although we sympathize with Margaret's loss and appreciate her grief, her response mechanisms are quirky and unusual enough to be funny. After learning that Cass is working as a staff member on the sensationalistic, trash-talking *Lamont Whipper Show*, Margaret becomes a regular viewer. Despite her conservative, PTA/Junior League tendencies, she braves stories of women having affairs with their sister's husbands and confrontations surrounding the topic "You're Too Fat to Be All That" just to maintain some connection to her daughter. The incongruity here is palpable. To replace the emptiness she feels, Margaret also begins to collect Victorian-era dolls that crop up in the most unexpected places around the house. One finds a home on the bathroom floor, causing Caitlin's father to shriek when he mistakes it for a toilet brush. Caitlin's mother spends time trying to decide how to organize them, debating whether or not to put the townsfolk in one place or break them into more intimate groups. We do not laugh at Margaret's pain but can find some lightness in her attempts to cope.

Rina's adventures in love provide another break from the weighty aspects of the story. Caitlin's best friend, Rina has watched her mother marry one man after the next, seeking not love but wealth and dragging her daughter from one home to another always in search of more square footage and better neighbors. Gorgeous, confident, and flirtatious, Rina is a heart-breaker who chases boys to compensate for the fact that her father refuses to claim her as his own. Her romantic exploits involve her in regular love triangles. The most recent involves herself, the high school quarterback, and a college-aged shoe salesman who continually flips his long, blonde bangs out of his face. Rina's saga provides not only a diversion but a contrasting story to Caitlin's. As Caitlin hears her friend's trials and tribulations, she can't help but make comparisons to her own life, wondering if there is any hope that she might one day enjoy such worries.

Even in the simple details of mundane living, Dessen manages to make us laugh and give us reassurance that all is not wrong with Caitlin's world. In preparation for the annual April Fool's party hosted by Caitlin's family and neighbors, Caitlin, her father, her mother, Boo, Stewart, and two fraternity brothers forced to serve time for misbehavior attempt to set up a large tent. In the dark, amidst bugs devouring their legs, the cursing of the frat boys, the subsequent reprimands of Caitlin's father, and Stewart's discussion of a barn-raising program he watched on public television, we are presented a highly comedic version of the event. Caitlin is happy to be present, remembering years before when she and Cass begged to remain outside just a few minutes longer, wanting the games of tag and kickball to never end. Despite the horror of her situation with her boyfriend, Caitlin holds on to parts of her earlier, happier self. Perhaps she can escape her nightmare and resume a reality that brings joy and comfort back into her life.

Symbols That Enrich and Amplify the Story

More so than in her other novels, Dessen draws upon rich symbolism to show the development of the primary female protagonist. In addition to Caitlin's scar and the dreamland metaphor discussed above, Dessen also utilizes everyday objects to embody the complexity of Caitlin's changing vision of self. The thin, silver bangles that occupy Corinna's wrists for most of the novel, for example, morph in meaning as Caitlin shifts in her development. The bracelets are given to

Corinna by her lazy boyfriend, Dave, who gives her a new bangle as a gift each Christmas, birthday, and Valentine's Day. The bracelets represent the bindings that trap Corinna in her unhealthy relationship, one that sees her as a possession held to a man who uses and defines her. When she removes them upon leaving Dave and heading to California, she is freed both literally and figuratively.

The sad irony, however, is that Caitlin finds the bracelets waiting for her in a bowl at the now-empty house and begins to wear them. She accepts the trappings of the unhealthy relationship Corinna has managed to escape and claims that even Corinna can't help her now. When she flees Rina's house later in the novel in a frantic attempt to get to Rogerson before he is fully angered at her, she notices the song of the bracelets guiding her into danger and follows their sound rather than turning back. The bracelets are both comforting and destructive, much like the relationship she and Corinna share. Even after the abuse ends and Caitlin begins her recovery, she refuses to remove the bracelets, even in the shower. At this point, however, they have transformed, just as she has. They no longer represent bondage but serve as a reminder of the girl she once was and never again wants to be.

Caitlin's photographs symbolize, too, the development of her character. Once the abuse begins, they represent Caitlin's attempt to keep the world sane given the chaos of her daily life with Rogerson. Photographs of family and friends allow her to lull herself into believing for a time the false assumption that "everything was still okay" (184). She hangs the portraits of family and friends around her room—Corinna on the front steps in the sunlight with her dog, Boo sitting cross-legged next to the cement Buddha in the grass of her backyard, her mother scanning the television in search of Cass' fleeting appearance, even Rogerson posing with every expression except the one that causes her to squeeze her eyes shut and bear down before each attack. Yet, even Caitlin realizes her photographs are skewed images of the truth. She studies them, realizing, "They stared back at me, frozen, but even though I could read their entire world in their faces, none of them were looking that closely at me" (185). Her escape into the world of photography is not enough to provide real solace.

Caitlin's photographs encourage her gradual recovery and provide her the power to heal as she works through the pain of her experiences once the abuse ends. At the outset of her treatment, she cannot face the girl she was, the one captured in the self-portrait she creates for her final project in her art class. This girl is flat, oblivious. She has "spent her whole life wanting to be someone else, something else, and it had gotten her nowhere" (227). She rips the self-portrait into several tiny pieces and gathers them into a bag hidden away in the front drawer of her desk. When she eventually begins the process of putting the pieces together again, she parallels her own need to rebuild the person she is given who she was. She needs to be made whole again, recognizing that the girl in the picture—stoned, bruised, and silent—remains a part of who she is and who she will become. Bit by bit, day by day, she assembles the mosaic and learns to love herself for all she is and will be.

Dreamland represents Dessen's greatest risk thus far in her career, one she doesn't take lightly. She recognizes the need to be careful and responsible when dealing with the issue of abuse, especially given the intended audience. "Teenage girls are evolving so much and it's so easy— the first time you fall in love especially—to think maybe this is just the way it's supposed to be, or 'Nobody will ever love me again.' You don't have the strength that you would have later, to walk away."[18] In its honest depiction of the destructive behaviors commonly exhibited by young women in relationships in which love has led to physical and emotional violence, her story may serve as the necessary catalyst for change.

Notes

1. Sarah Dessen, "*Dreamland*," *Personal Website*, at www.sarahdessen.com/dreamland.html (accessed 4 March 2003).

2. Dessen, "*Dreamland*," *Personal Website*.

3. Dessen, "*Dreamland*," *Personal Website*.

4. Ilene Cooper, review of *Dreamland*, by Sarah Dessen, *Booklist* 97, 1 November 2000.

5. Patty Campbell, review of *Dreamland*, by Sarah Dessen, *Amazon.com* (accessed 28 May 2004).

6. Gail Richmond, review of *Dreamland*, by Sarah Dessen, *School Library Journal* 46, September 2000, 221.

7. Review of *Dreamland*, by Sarah Dessen, *The Horn Book*, September/October 2000.

8. Review of *Dreamland*, by Sarah Dessen, *Kirkus Reviews*, 15 July 2000.

9. Patty Campbell, *Dreamland: A Reader's Companion* (New York: Viking, 2000).

10. Campbell, *Amazon.com*.

11. Cooper, *Booklist*.

12. Campbell, *Dreamland: A Reader's Companion*.

13. Cooper, *Booklist*.

14. Don Gallo, "Interview with Sarah Dessen," *authors4teens*, at www
.authors4teens.com/index.asp (accessed 2 April 2004).

15. Cooper, *Booklist*.

16. *Kirkus Reviews*.

17. Dessen, "*Dreamland*," *Personal Website*.

18. Campbell, *Dreamland: A Reader's Companion*.

CHAPTER SEVEN

~

The Strains and Refrains
of *This Lullaby*

"In the depth of winter, I finally learned that within me there lay an invincible summer" (Camus in front matter). *This Lullaby*, Dessen's fifth novel, explores the theme of necessary faith in love. Unlike Dessen's other novels which explore romantic relationships in the context of other issues, this novel has love at its core. After writing *Dreamland*, which Dessen describes as "so heavy, so emotional," she wished to undertake something "a little lighter, but that still had something to say."[1] The resulting story is about "coming to terms with the fact that loving someone requires a leap of faith, and that a soft landing is never guaranteed."[2] Despite botched relationships, broken hearts, and romance-induced anxieties and stresses, believing in love is worth the risk. Although the trials of romantic relationships may leave us feeling cold and alone, even the hardest of hearts can be softened. An ALA Best Book for Young Adults, an Original Voices Selection for the Borders Group, a New York Public Library Book for the Teen Age, and a *Los Angeles Times* Book Prize Finalist, *This Lullaby* has been well-received. With "insightful writing,"[3] the "wry, humorous voice"[4] of the protagonist, and a "cast of idiosyncratic characters who watch from the sidelines,"[5] the novel reflects Dessen's continuing success as an author. Dessen, too, feels good about the book, noting that the process was a bit like "riding a comet."

A self-professed cynic in the world of love, eighteen-year-old Remy has experienced the loss of a father who abandoned her before she was born and has suffered through four of her mother's remarriages and soon-to-follow divorces. She is indeed in the winter of love and claims she has a cold heart as a result. In the summer following high school graduation, she wants nothing more than to spend quality time with her three girlfriends—Lissa, Jess, and Chloe—find a short-term boyfriend who will provide one last fling, and depart for Stanford with no entanglements, ready to begin a new life away from the responsibility of having to care for her hopelessly naive mother. Remy does not count upon the arrival of Dexter, however, a clumsy singer in a rock band who, during their first meeting, claims that he and Remy are meant to be together. Despite Remy's best attempts to keep Dexter from knowing her as more than the bitchy girl with the hard exterior, she lets him get close, thus complicating her desire to end the summer relationship-free. Remy is forced to face her fears regarding love and admit that, perhaps, taking a risk on the heart is worth the potential heartbreak.

"A Crazy Little Thing Called Love"

Remy is surrounded by a cast of romantics pitted against her cynicism, a tactic Dessen employs with skill and intention. As a protagonist, Remy differs from the teen speakers who appear in Dessen's other novels. Before starting *This Lullaby*, Dessen feared she would repeat herself and create a story too similar to her earlier tales. She struggled with voice and wondered if there was anything new for her to share. To provide a solution, her agent noted that Dessen's protagonists tend to be "serious, thoughtful girls with dynamic, wild friends"[6] and that perhaps Dessen should write from the perspective of one of the friends for a change. Dessen's original reaction to this suggestion was that of disbelief. How could she, the wall-hugger, the shy girl with the loud friends, get into the head of this kind of character? With time, however, Remy's voice became clearer and has come to represent Dessen's id, providing an outlet that allows Dessen to say what she has always wished to but never has. For Dessen, Remy has a "hard edge to her. She's been hurt, she's wised up to a lot of things, and she handles guys in a very assertive way. On the flip side, she's really shut off emotionally. . . . She's traded her heart, in many ways, for her strength, without realizing that she can have both."[7]

"Love Stinks"

In matters of love, Remy holds no illusions. She believes that "it came, it went, it left casualties or it didn't. People weren't meant to be together forever, regardless of what the songs say" (57). Love can leave us as victims, weakened as a result of having trusted in someone who eventually lets us down. When Remy learns that her boyfriend, Jonathan, has cheated on her, her greatest pain results not from the fact that the relationship ended but that she looks like a fool for having believed in the relationship in the first place. When she allows Dexter to hold her after a drunken episode at a local bar, she is later angered by her lack of resolve, claiming, "I didn't show weakness: I didn't depend on anyone" (117). Remy is frustrated, too, by the weakness she sees in her mother, Barbara, who seems to neglect her own desires in hopes of making Don, her newest beau, happy. Barbara allows him to interrupt her previously sacred writing routine, for example. For Remy, love should not require sacrifice or having to settle. She wonders if her perception would be different had she lived in a home where a stable marriage existed. Based on her experiences, love, quite simply, does not work. Remy is confident she has deciphered the puzzle of love and wants nothing to do with the pain she believes ultimately results from any romantic relationship. Dessen, who says she couldn't wait to prove Remy wrong, forces her to question her stance by contrasting her views of love with those of several other characters.

"Love Is a Many-Splendored Thing"

Although Remy believes she has learned how not to love from her mother, her mother believes in love, even if she possesses an overly-idealized view of the notion. Barbara Starr asserts that love requires some level of compromise in order to last. Barbara admits that Don has his share of annoying habits and behaviors but tells Remy that he is a good man, arguing that the love they share compensates for these small differences. Although she has not had much success in marriage, Barbara values the relationships she has experienced. She recognizes that she has been hurt but tells Remy that, more importantly, she has loved and been loved. "Holding people away from you, and denying yourself love," she tells Remy, "doesn't make you strong. If anything, it makes you weaker" (265). We must not fear the process of taking a chance, of taking a risk. Even when Don turns out to be an adulterer, Barbara's faith in love remains unshaken. Just a few hours after she learns the truth about Don, she shares her joy at the news of her son's engagement, expressing a genuine belief in "the love stories she not only wrote but lived" (319).

"All You Need Is Love"
Chris and Dexter are united in that they could easily share Remy's cynicism regarding romance but choose to believe in love instead. As Remy's brother, Chris has experienced the same arrival and departure of Barbara's many men. He and Remy, in fact, have made a habit of placing bets at the start of each marriage, wagering on the amount of time it will take for the relationship to fall apart. For a time, Remy says Chris was the only one who shared her views on love. They had always told one another that they would never get married, "no way, shoot me if I do" (97). With the arrival of his girlfriend, Jennifer Anne, however, Chris changes his mind. He finds love and now tells Remy that she is missing out. When Remy asks him what made him decide to take a risk on Jennifer Anne, especially considering the heartbreak that he has witnessed, he tells her that the decision was not calculated, not like making a financial investment. Remy states that she just doesn't get it. With Dexter, too, Remy finds it hard to believe that he can maintain faith in love. His mother is on her fifth marriage, an impressive record even in Remy's eyes. Given their shared history, Remy thinks Dexter is crazy to think that forever is possible. Dexter reinforces metaphorically the comments of Barbara and Chris. While working at the local photo developing lab, he is given a shipment of defective cameras to use as he sees fit. Remy thinks any time spent snapping pictures with faulty cameras is a waste. Dexter tells her, however, that perhaps the pictures will turn out just fine. They will not know unless they try. "Maybe they won't be perfect—I mean, they could be blurred, or cut off in the middle—but I'm thinking it's worth a shot" (260). For Remy, the odds are just not good enough.

"Endless Love"
Remy's friend Lissa serves as a foil to Remy's character. She is romantic and emotional, continuing to love the boy who dumps her, crying at

weddings, and opening herself up to heartbreak in the search for love. While Remy sees relationships as a crutch, a foolish need for someone else, Lissa embraces this need. She defines love as "putting up with someone's bad qualities because they somehow complete you" (248). She reminds Remy that she overlooked Dexter's untied shoelaces, clumsiness, and messy room—all faults that typically serve to annoy Remy and her sense of order. She identifies and names Remy's emotions in a way that strikes a chord, telling her, "Dexter was the closest you've ever come to love. . . . It was close. Real close. You could have loved him" (250). Remy's reply? "No way. Not a chance" (250). Ever the believer, Lissa calls Remy on her outward display of callousness in love, arguing that Remy has always believed in love, that her faith has not been lost but misplaced. She has been looking in the wrong places for the love that she desperately craves. It is not lost forever, just waiting to be found.

Relinquishing Control

"Take a Chance on Me"

This misplaced faith in love is found in Remy's relationship with Dexter. It is through her evolving encounters with him that Remy comes to see the wisdom of the romantics who surround her. Remy must learn to see herself in a new light, to accept her real self rather than hide behind the identity she has created as a protective mechanism. With his carefree demeanor and accepting ways, Dexter disrupts her plans and teaches her that love is sometimes beyond our control. He knocks down her "carefully constructed defenses as their rocky romance progresses."[8] Even Dessen admits to falling for Dexter in her creation of him, especially his "absolute carefree faith in things turning out okay."[9]

Remy prides herself on the order she has created in her life. She keeps her closet neat and tidy, her room perfectly organized, and her car free from all food and beverages. Her desire for control extends into her love life, as well. In matters of the heart, she has been burned too many times to leave things up to chance. According to Dessen, Remy "wants hard proof, facts, a mathematical equation where X equals Y, before she'll even begin to think about taking any kind of risk."[10] Not only has she suffered the loss of a father and several stepfathers, she has been hurt in her personal relationships, as well. After getting drunk and being raped by an older student at a party, Remy allowed herself, for a time, to lose control as a coping mechanism. She dated one boy after the other, drinking with abandon and engaging in promiscuous sex, seeking love in the form of physical affection.

Unable to find the solace she sought, Remy no longer wishes to be that girl. She now chooses her boyfriends carefully, ensuring that each fits an acceptable profile—nice face, good body, and easy to dump when the right time comes. She still has sex with them but on her terms. Once she knows they are not in the relationship for the long haul and she does not have to worry about commitment, she is willing to sleep with them. Remy has a relationship schedule that keeps others from getting too close. After the first six weeks of blind euphoria in a new relationship, the cracks begin to show, and beau behaviors that were once endearing become annoying. It is then time for The Speech, Remy's tool for slowing things down and making it clear that the relationship will not lead to anything serious. This pattern allows her to remain safe, insulated from heartbreak, and in charge.

Dexter disrupts her pattern. The "antithesis of her usual guy: clumsy, messy, impetuous, and persistent, but, worst of all, a musician,"[11] Dexter is not willing to play the role Remy has formulated for him. He tests her continually, forcing her to alter and eventually abandon her relationship formula. She opts not to give him The Speech, does not sleep with him, and, perhaps most significantly, allows him to eat in her car. In a humorous scene early in their relationship, Remy gives Dexter a ride home. Although she warns him repeatedly about her no-food-in-the-car policy, he removes a greasy French fry from his bag and conducts an experiment, laying the fry on the gearshift console and telling Remy not to panic and to appreciate instead "the freedom in this chaos" for just a moment (87). Although Remy remains outwardly unemotional throughout the ordeal, Dexter's audacity charms her. Physically, too, Remy cannot control Dexter and his nervous energy. Despite her attempts to calm his ever-bouncing knees and drumming fingers, she is unable to silence them and, instead, finds herself getting caught up in his movement, "jangling along, as if whatever current charged him was now flowing through [her]" (126).

Although Remy prides herself on her brash, don't-give-a-damn-what-you-think-of-me façade, Dexter is able to break through to the real girl underneath. He describes her as sweet when she buys him and his poor housemates a set of eating utensils and calls her a big softie who is nice to his dog, helps him separate colors from whites, and resolves a conflict over an unpaid electric bill. His description of her leaves Remy feeling "strangely unnerved," as if he has discovered a secret she did not even know she was keeping (189). She cares what he thinks of her, choosing not to sleep with him out of fear that he might think less of her. And she is possessive of him when another girl admires him during the band's performance at a local club, feeling protective when she is not even sure she wants the thing she is trying to protect. In each instance, Remy allows Dexter some control over her perception of self, relinquishing her need to maintain a tough, impenetrable heart.

Although Remy briefly ends her relationship with Dexter, claiming it is simpler for them to be apart as she will be departing for college soon, she is not the same person she was. He has changed her. She begins a final fling with a college student named Paul. He is dubbed Perfect Paul due to his good looks, generous gift-giving habits, and, most significantly, acceptance of the fact that the relationship is all in fun and will last for just a few weeks. He fits Remy's profile, but the profile no longer suits her. She misses Dexter's gangly elbows, untied shoes, and genuine love. She even begins to value romantic gestures. She envies her mother's urgent need to get home to tell Don that she wants their marriage to work, admitting, "it was nice, this rushing need to say something to someone right this very second. Almost romantic, really" (293). Remy could easily leave for Stanford without having to cross paths with Dexter, but something about him nags her. He is a loose end that she is unable to tie up. Against her nature, she makes the choice to go to him, to take a risk. She recognizes the fact that her earlier beliefs about love resulted in nothing more than "[a] string of boyfriends. A reputation as a cold, bitter bitch. And a secure bubble that I'd drawn so tightly around myself that no one, not even someone with the best of intentions, could get in, even if I wanted them to" (334). Once afraid to take a chance on love, Remy learns that love requires faith in the unknown, that, as Dessen describes, "the living is in the leaping. Sometimes, you just have to close your eyes, and jump."[12]

"Love Will Keep Us Together"

Remy's control issues extend into her relationship with her mother, as well. In her interactions with her mom, Remy assumes the identity of the one in charge, the one with all the answers, the one who resolves every crisis. Remy describes herself as her mother's business manager, therapist, handyman, and wedding coordinator. She has a penchant for dealing with the complexities of her mother's life. Her mother wants to be in on the fun but only when her involvement results in little inconvenience or stress for her. She loves to dive into projects but rarely sees anything through, leaving Remy to pick up the pieces and clean up the mess. The aromatherapy kits, family tree software, Japanese cookbooks, and algae-covered aquarium that take up space throughout the house attest to Barbara's whims.

Although it seems that Remy resents the responsibility she must assume for her mother, she finds comfort in being needed. While her mother naps away the afternoon on the day after Remy's graduation, Remy takes care of last-minute wedding plans. She experiences a burning in her stomach each time she feels used by her mother but, at the same time, prides herself on her efficiency and ability to defuse any crisis. When the limo service is unable to pick up the family on the night of Barbara and Don's rehearsal dinner, Remy takes the phone from her hysterical mother and makes alternate arrangements. At the family Fourth of July cookout when her mother insists on expensive Brazilian steaks prepared on a state-of-the-art grill, Remy anticipates the burnt meat and brings out the hamburger patties she purchased and hid in the back of the freezer just in case. When Remy learns of Don's affair and the impending divorce, she moves into crisis management mode and informs her mother that they will need to contact the bank, the lawyer, etc. She assumes that her mother continues to need her. In this final instance, however, Remy is denied her role.

With this turn of events, mother and daughter are changed. For the first time, Remy's mother steps up and offers to handle the dilemma herself. She tells her daughter that she has assumed responsibility for her mother long enough and that it is now time for Remy to worry about herself. Remy's first reaction is to be offended. How can her mother not need her when this is what she does best? She then experiences fear, realizing:

This was it, what I'd always wanted. The official out, the moment I was finally set free. But it didn't feel the way I'd thought it would. Instead of a wash of victory, I felt strangely alone, as if everything fell away suddenly, leaving me with only the sound of my heart beating. It scared me. (315)

In losing control over her mother's life, part of her established identity falls away. Remy needs her mother (and her regular crises) to maintain her perception of self. Without the responsibility of having to care for Barbara, Remy is left only to care for herself. Barbara's decision to assert control over her own life frees Remy to begin to live hers. Although afraid, Remy accepts her mother's offer for escape, forgiving and thanking her mother at the same time.

Friends to the End

Remy's primary support system is the circle of girlfriends who surround her, offering guidance, advice, and a good laugh just when needed. Whether they are hanging out at the local convenience mart drinking Zip diets or trading stories and dreams at The Spot, their private hideout, the four young women share a powerful bond.

Lissa is sentimental and traditional. Of the four, she is the only one who cries at her high school graduation and is dreading the end of summer when she and her friends will part ways, each pursuing a different path. Lissa plans to attend the local university, the spires of the church in her old neighborhood visible from her dorm room window. She assumes she and her high school sweetheart, the only boy with whom she has had sex, will live in dorms that are near one another, share a few classes, and continue their relationship unabated. According to Remy, Lissa "felt things too deeply" (22). As a result, Remy feels most protective of her and most guilty about leaving her in a few short weeks.

Jess is solid and dependable. Upon the death of her mother, she assumes the role of caregiver for her two younger brothers. She is never late; she never drinks or smokes; she always drives. Remy knows she is one of the few people who will not put up with any foolishness. She tells it like it is. A large but not overweight girl, able to throw a dodgeball with greater force than most of the boys her age, Jess is often seen as mean. Her friends know better, however, understanding that her financial and familial circumstances have hastened her maturity.

Chloe is wild and sarcastic. She drives a Mercedes and is always dressed in the latest styles. Her mother, a flight attendant who is often away, brings back fashions from Paris and Milan and keeps a fully-stocked liquor cabinet of tiny airline bottles of gin, vodka, and rum. Remy calls Chloe "our little trendsetter" (26). Like Remy, Chloe is honest and forthright and, in matters of the heart, shares Remy's cut and dry "love 'em and leave 'em" attitude toward relationships (194). She is drawn to college-aged men who cheat on her and is content to avoid commitment and have fun while she is still young enough to do so.

Despite their varied personalities, these friends have developed relationships with one another that remain strong and true. They are able to laugh at one another. Jess and Chloe provide a running banter regarding the size of Chloe's breasts, Jess commenting repeatedly on whether Chloe even needs a bra and Chloe defending repeatedly her small, but adequate, breast size. Lissa, Jess, and Chloe are comfortable enough in their relationship with Remy to tease her about her high expectations regarding boyfriends. When Remy reveals that it is time to dump another boy, each girl pipes in with a speculative reason for his downfall—declaring undying love, wearing a nonmatching outfit, making a major grammatical error, or arriving fifteen minutes late. The friends are also willing to defend one another. Their weapon of choice is the Zip drink, which works remarkably well as a projectile missile. When Remy, Jess, and Lissa see Adam, the boy who breaks Lissa's heart, smiling in the parking lot of a local coffee shop, they circle around, take aim, and douse him in a cold, icy beverage tossed with great precision from their moving car. A repeat performance occurs when the girls run into Don after Remy learns of his affair. Most importantly, the girls care deeply about one another. When Remy suffers a tough day, visits a local bar, has too much to drink, and has to fend off assault charges, Jess picks her up and expresses her anger, showing concern that something could have happened to her friend. When Lissa takes to driving down the street of her old flame and finds herself hurting when she learns that he is seeing someone new, the girls give stern advice on the need for her to let him go. Even when it will put a strain on their relationship, the girls support one another. When Remy is hesitant to express her feelings for Dexter, Lissa, Jess, and even Chloe, urge her forward, knowing that their friend has found real love and wanting her to be happy.

Heartbreakers and Heartthrobs

The men in this novel are divided by their commitment to the ones they profess to love. Dessen's portrayal of the varied males leads us to admire those who stay and condemn those who flee. The gentle romantics are celebrated, while those selfish in love are derided.

"These Boots Are Made for Walking"

Thomas Custer, Remy's father, quite simply abandons his wife and family. A hippie musician with no claim to fame, he heads to California, leaving behind his pregnant wife and son. When he receives word of Remy's birth, he composes his one hit song, "This Lullaby," while strumming his guitar for an hour at the local Motel 6. He dies from a heart attack two years later, having never attempted to meet the daughter who provided him his only notoriety. Remy sees his song as a lie, a chance for her father to scribble some words and notes on a page and attain redemption for his behavior, "his words living forever, while [she] was left speechless, no rebuttal, no words left to say" (163). "I will let you down," his lyrics promise, and he delivers (163).

Don Davis, husband number five and head of Davis Motors, opts to leave only when an affair with his secretary is discovered. At first, he is seemingly thrilled about his impending marriage to Barbara, circling the date on the calendar like a boy anticipating a holiday. Once married, however, he shows little respect for his new wife, leaving his empty weight-loss shake cans throughout the house, demanding that she bring him a beer, interrupting her while she is trying to write, and, most tellingly, using Barbara's bed as the site of his indiscretions, namely sleeping with his secretary and photographing her in a provocative pose to commemorate the event. When confronted, he simply sighs and heads to the bedroom to pack his bags. Remy believes that this says much about his remorse. She wonders what kind of car salesman does not at least try to talk his way out of a bad situation.

"Our Love Is Here to Stay"

Chris and Dexter once again share common ground in that they are depicted admirably due to their faith in love. Each young man is committed to the object of his affection despite the fact that the loving relationships they have witnessed have generally turned sour. Chris, a former drug dealer, is reformed after a bit of jail time and the arrival of Jennifer Anne, his highly organized, ambitious girlfriend. Remy sees a changed man in Chris. He dresses better, works harder, and uses proper grammar as a result of Jennifer Anne's influence. His resulting commitment to her is obvious when he defends Jennifer Anne and her sometimes prudish and trite ways in the face of Remy's disparaging, wry wit. Although he and Remy are close, he refuses to let her destroy the love that he has found.

Dexter demonstrates a level of commitment to Remy that some may argue she does not deserve. Although she gives him the cold shoulder, tells him to go away, and, after they have grown close, dumps him, Dexter remains true. When Dexter and Remy run into one another at the local convenience mart, Dexter questions Remy on her motives, accusing her of never loving him but wanting him to be like every other guy in her string of short-term boyfriends. For Dexter, however, the relationship meant and still means more. He tells Remy, "I wasn't playing some kind of summer game. Everything I said was true, from the very first day" (289). This young man doesn't care why Remy loves him, only that she does, and truly believes they were meant to be together.

Laughter in Love

This Lullaby is replete with laughable moments. Where love is concerned, human behavior provides fertile ground for the comic's wit. Dessen has taken up the charge with great skill.

With the arrival of Don comes Don's furniture, enough to destroy even the healthiest of relationships. Looming large in the master bedroom is Don's enormous, Moroccan tapestry that depicts various scenes from the Bible, the beheading of John the Baptist serving as Remy's favorite. Disturbing and offensive, it remains in the room only because the thread color matches the carpet, a generous compromise on the part of Remy's mother. Don also contributes a Renaissance-era painting of a heavy, busty woman posing in a garden, her breasts spilling out over the couch on which she lies. Hanging on the wall behind the kitchen table, the painting inspires Chris to comment on the fact that each breast must have weighed a good five to seven pounds. Then there is the modern art statue that bears a close resemblance to a penis, not to mention the red leather sofa which "screamed Single Man on the Make" (124). This composite portrait of the man and his furnishings says much about his character while making us chuckle.

The salon in which Remy works provides several humorous incidents that provide a light-hearted look at the extremes to which women will go to look attractive in hopes of acquiring love. One afternoon, patrons hear, "Aiiiieeeeeee! . . . Mother of pearl! . . . Oh, suuu-ugggaaarrr! . . . and H-E-double-hockey-sticks!" shouted by Mrs. Michaels, the wife of a local minister in for her regular bikini wax. According to Remy, she "loved God almost as much as having a smooth, hairless body" (45). As Mrs. Michaels walks stiffly out of the salon, Remy notes the irony of the fact that the patrons look like war victims after their beauty treatments. Beauty is pain. This is demonstrated in a later scene in which a woman is having her hair colored. At first, she calls out tentatively to her stylist, "my scalp is burning." Her voice then becomes more nervous in tone, "It's really hurting." Now screaming, ready to cry, she howls, "I think I smell burning hair." She now has the attention of the stylist who, angry at being interrupted in conversation, heads over to assess the situation. After the scalp is bandaged, a gift certificate is given, and a promise for lifelong eyebrow waxing is made, the episode ends, and we are left laughing.

Dexter's band, Truth Squad, also contributes much to the humor of the novel. Despite their inability to take care of the most mundane household tasks, like paying the electric bill and doing their laundry, they have a penchant for composing inspirational lyrics for their collection of love songs, dubbed the Potato Opus. The songs are based upon a relationship gone awry in which the female dumps the male due to his meat-eating tendencies after her choice to assume a vegan lifestyle. They contain such touching lines as:

She'd given up the cheese and bacon, sworn off Burger King, and when
I wouldn't do the same she gave me back my ring. . . . Don't you ever

give me no rotten tomato, 'cause all I ever wanted was your sweet potato. Mashed, whipped, creamed, smothered, chunked, and diced, anyway you fix it baby sure tastes nice. (140–41)

This is then followed by a litany of any and every possible kind of vegetable and a climactic cymbal crash. A love song for all time.

The Crafting of Character

Dessen demonstrates skill as a writer in her ability to weave several underlying motifs into the basic plot line of *This Lullaby*. In the development of Remy and Barbara, she incorporates two art forms—music and
the novel—to achieve a richness and depth that could not be achieved
through descriptive details of character alone.

"I Have to Say I Love You in a Song"
This novel is infused with music. There is the music piped into the
lobby of Don Davis Motors, the company theme song that Dexter
claims will be he and Remy's song. There is the music of Barbara's typewriter, a percussive fingers-upon-keys sound that defines Remy's memories of childhood. There is the music of Dexter's band, Truth Squad,
their rehearsals and club performances setting the backdrop for the developing romantic relationship between Dexter and Remy. And, most
importantly, there is the music of the lullaby, the song composed by
Remy's father that both haunts and comforts her and reflects her developing attitude toward love.

Remy describes the lullaby as the one constant in her life, the one
thing that remains steady in her world of revolving stepfathers and
boyfriends. She says, "The recording never changed, the words staying
the same, my father's voice taking the same breaths between lines"
(227). The recording remains hidden in her CD player in the back of
her closet, ready to offer condolence when her life seems too painful.
She alone knows how much she needs the song, that it does mean
something to her despite her feelings regarding her father and his absence. When Dexter's band plays the song during a performance in a
"self-mocking" way as if it is "winking at its own seriousness," Remy is
hurt and confused (209). To others, the song is just an old, sappy tune

of their parents' era, while, for Remy, the song has so much weight that it has the power to drown her. The fact that Dexter knows how she feels about the song but chooses to sing it anyway is particularly painful. The notes, now "twisted and different," are sung, Remy explains, by "another man I hardly knew who had some claim to me, however small" (210). The parallel to her father is too close, as Remy fears that Dexter will hurt her just the same. As she learns to trust Dexter and her own ability to love despite the potential consequences, the song, ultimately, takes on a new and greater meaning. With Dexter's changed lyrics—"Even if I let you down"—the song reminds Remy that, in love, there are no guarantees and that that is okay.

"Stand By Your Man"?

Dessen also uses a literary technique to trace the development of Barbara's character and her musings regarding marriage. Dessen creates a story within a story, using Barbara's latest romance novel as a countermelody that allows Barbara to express her thoughts regarding her newest relationship. In Barbara's tale, we follow Melanie, a spunky and vivacious woman who loves a challenge, especially when it comes to romance. When she crosses paths with Brock Dobbin, a former lover from whom she parted on less than ideal terms, she goes to meet him at the Plaza Hotel to put him in his place and tell him of her choice to marry the stalwart, dependable Luc Perethel. Barbara, like Melanie, is ready to dive into her marriage, believing that all will be well. She tells Remy that "it feels real this time. Permanent" (57). Soon thereafter, however, Melanie's marriage bed leaves her cold, and she wonders if her decision to choose Luc over Brock, reason over passion, was a mistake. Barbara, too, expresses her doubts about her own marriage when she asks Remy about the costs of settling for less than one desires. When Melanie and Brock meet again at a cafe later in the novel, he tries to win her back, professing his love for her. She remains with Luc, however, claiming that she will make the marriage work even if Luc cannot love her like Brock once had and can again. Brock was forever leaving—going on assignment, chasing a story, disappearing repeatedly. Melanie wants stability. Like Melanie, Barbara wants "to believe in a forever. Even one that sometimes left her wanting at night, dreaming of better things" (278). In order to make the relationship with Don last, she must compromise her expectations of love. In the end, Melanie opts for no man, leaving Luc and the security he provides and refusing to be hurt by Brock despite her attraction to him. She boards the train alone and hopes to forge a future on her own. Barbara, too, has acquired a confidence that requires that she find herself before she can lose herself in another relationship.

This Lullaby has allowed Dessen to stray from her usual voice and explore the perspective of the outspoken cynic, the girl who knows what she believes and is willing to vocalize her emotions—at least on the surface. However, like the other female protagonists Dessen has brought to life, Remy is reluctant to look deeply into herself and see herself for who she is. Even those who appear resilient and unable to break can bend under the weightiness of life and love.

Notes

1. Sarah Dessen, "*This Lullaby*," *Personal Website*, at www.sarahdessen.com/thislullaby.html (accessed 4 March 2003).

2. Miranda Doyle, review of *This Lullaby*, by Sarah Dessen, *School Library Journal*, April 2002.

3. Review of *This Lullaby*, by Sarah Dessen, *Kirkus Reviews*, 15 April 2002.

4. Doyle, *School Library Journal*.

5. Diane Roback, Jennifer M. Brown, and Jason Britten, review of *This Lullaby*, by Sarah Dessen, *Publishers Weekly*, 20 May 2002.

6. "An Interview with Sarah Dessen," *Razorbill*, at www.razorbillzine.com/interviewsd.html (accessed 4 March 2003).

7. "An Interview with Sarah Dessen," *Razorbill*.

8. Doyle, *School Library Journal*.

9. "An Interview with Sarah Dessen," *Razorbill*.

10. Dessen, "*This Lullaby*," *Personal Website*.

11. *Kirkus Reviews*.

12. Dessen, "*This Lullaby*," *Personal Website*.

~

CHAPTER EIGHT

Chaos, Control, and
The Truth About Forever

"If your forever was ending tomorrow, would this be how you'd want to spend it?" (136). Dessen's newest novel, *The Truth About Forever* (2004), asks a hard question of readers: are you really living or just going through the motions? The novel advocates the idea that, to live fully, we must accept the chaos that surrounds us rather than fight, deny, or attempt to control it. Life is achieved in the living, not seeking a predetermined future or becoming mired in events of a fixed past. According to Dessen, the story is ultimately about how "life is a continuing series of beginnings and endings, losses and gains, all folding into one long stretch, one lifetime, and one forever."[1]

For Dessen, the novel was a labor of love, the result of several false starts and arduous writing. Dessen describes feeling pressured to write a story to match the success attained by her earlier works. She finds this ironic in that the novel is about a girl who must learn to accept that perfection is not possible. She recalls the many times she said to her husband, "I'm writing a book about how it's OK to be imperfect, and I want it to be perfect."[2] With its intricate layers and rich symbolism, the novel is her most complex yet. Dessen believes that it was the most difficult to write, saying, "I've never been so immersed in the writing of a book before, and I had a hard time pulling myself away from it, even when I most wanted to."[3] The critics argue that Dessen "gracefully balances comedy with tragedy and introduces a complex heroine worth getting to know"[4] and that "at its purest, the writing roaches directly into the hearts of teenage girls,"[5] thus suggesting that these difficulties were worth the struggle.

Macy is a well-adjusted kid until a fateful morning on which she opts for a few more minutes of rest before joining her father on their routine jog. This short delay haunts Macy after she finds her father lying on the sidewalk suffering a fatal heart attack. If only . . . , she wonders. To cope with her loss, Macy turns inward, isolating herself from her former friends, quitting the track team, shutting out her mother and sister, and avoiding anything that might result in loss or heartache. She finds comfort in the attention of Jason, a boy she sees as perfect due to his clearly delineated plan for the future. Jason has all the answers, an essential for Macy, given all of her questions. While Jason attends camp for the summer, Macy agrees to work as his replacement at the library information desk, a job she finds tedious. Her remaining hours are spent preparing for the SATs, waiting for Jason's email messages, and ironing her shirts in preparation for the next day. In a twist of fate, however, Macy finds herself working for Wish Catering under the guidance of Delia and her motley crew. As Macy develops unlikely friendships and learns to risk personal connection once again, she begins to heal. She works through her relationship with her mother (who remains in denial about the loss of her husband) and Jason (who offers false solace) while finding a soul mate in Wes (a tattooed artist who helps her break down the walls she has built around herself).

The Faulty Pursuit of Perfection

Macy strives for perfection as a means to assert dominance over her life. Her father's death was too unpredictable, too unexplainable, an anomaly. If she can just remain in control, she believes, she can keep other things from going wrong. Macy plays the part of strong survivor, saying, "If I wanted people to see me as calm and collected, together, I had to look the part" (17). She parts and reparts her hair to ensure that it is just right before going out in public, wears makeup to conceal any imperfections, and spends half an hour curling and recurling her eyelashes to make sure each is lifted and separated just as it should be.

Macy realizes, however, that this is an act. She admits that she feels scared and angry but keeps these emotions as her own, something she can control when her world seems to be spinning. She refuses to grieve, as, in her mind, that would reveal weakness. Even when she wants to talk about her dad and how much she misses him, she refuses to open up. She believes that she has been doing so well for so long that admitting her pain would result in a failure of sorts. Despite her hard exterior, Macy regrets not allowing herself to mourn, wishing she had sobbed like her sister Caroline rather than jumping from shocked to just fine. Yet, Macy refuses to express her feelings or get too attached to anything or anyone, believing that loss is inevitable.

With the arrival of the caterers (and their embodiment of all things chaotic), Macy's predictable world is transformed. Macy meets Delia and her workers at an event hosted by her mother, a developer promoting a new neighborhood she has designed. The party is far from perfect, with drinks being spilled on guests, not enough appetizers, and a crash in the kitchen. Macy is intrigued by the craziness of it all, however, and is drawn to the kitchen where she finds herself recruited to work as a temporary cook in charge of cheese puffs and crab cakes. Although Delia offers her a job, Macy knows she must remain committed to her work at the library information desk. Yet, curiosity pulls her back to Delia and her offer. Macy is not a spontaneous person, but, on a whim, she follows the catering van once she spots it in traffic on the night she learns that Jason wants to put their relationship on hold. Macy's moonlighting begins.

Macy loves the madness of catering—from men pinching her butt to collisions that result in food down her shirt. At the end of each night, she finds herself strangely calmed by the chaos, completely unlike that which she feels while working at the library. In the rush of her work as a server, she sees herself as someone else: "a girl with her hair mussed, a stained shirt, smelling of whatever had been spilled or smeared on me. It was like Cinderella in reverse: if I was a princess for my daylight hours, at night I let myself and my composure go, just until the stroke of midnight, when I turned back to princess again, just in time" (105).

The caterers, who by now have become her friends, inspire in Macy a willingness to question what she has come to believe about herself and the world after her father's death. After experiencing yet another bout of humiliation under the critical eyes of Amanda and Bethany, her seemingly perfect coworkers at the library, Macy accepts that she will never be able to meet the expectations they hold for her. She tires of playing the game, sees that life is fleeting, and accepts an invitation from her catering friends to enjoy a night on the town. This is a night of revelation, as the truth about what happened that fateful morning a few years back is confirmed by a loud mouth at a local party. Macy is no longer able to hide the secret she has kept from her new friends out of fear that they, like everyone else, will see her as simply the girl who saw her father die. As a result of this revelation, both nothing and everything change. Her new friends remain as ever, offering support without pity or sadness, but Macy learns that holding back bits of herself results in the denial of her identity.

Macy continues to progress. On a particularly long day at the library when Amanda and Bethany have relegated Macy to the back room to sort old magazines, Wes comes by with a question regarding the location of the catering tongs. Know-it-alls that they are, Amanda and Bethany assume they have the answer and push Wes to ask them instead. They are obviously humiliated when they not only do not have the answer but learn that Macy does. Macy has had enough and quits the job, opting to hop over the counter in her final farewell rather than scramble through their usual barricade of chairs. She leaves without regret. Macy spends her first night of freedom at another catering job, one in which all goes surprisingly smoothly. The food is prepared without any disaster, the carts all fit into the van, a lost serving platter is found, the caterers arrive early to the gig, the gas grills are not broken as had been thought, and there is extra food on hand. This unexpected lack of chaos reveals just how much Macy has changed. She realizes that, before, this predictability, this surety, was desirable to her. Now, it is simply boring.

The real test of Macy's growth, however, emerges on the ambulance ride to the hospital in the face of Delia's impending delivery of her second child. This trip, this journey, parallels Macy's earlier ride with her father. This one will result in life, while the other signified death. The sounds of the emergency room doors, the sanitized smell, the fear is all there. At first, Macy feels too haunted by the past, unable to cope with the present. She cannot sit still in the waiting room, as the memories of her last visit to this place shake her at the core. Yet, when she looks in the new baby's eyes, she is calmed, wondering what it is like to start fresh and see the world as new. Realizing all she has lost in her unwillingness to mourn, Macy finally allows herself to grieve as she should have the first time around. She sobs, letting the tears flow, and, more significantly, accepting the consolation and supportive arms of Wes, who holds her while she gives in to her sadness and pain. Rather than pulling back and into herself, she opens up. Loss "can either make you fearful or fearless."[6] In the end, under the guidance of a most unlikely support network, Macy has become a little less afraid of being imperfect, of reaching out to others, of being herself.

Reevaluating Her Relationships

Macy's growth is evidenced by the changing relationships she shares with those in her life. Her choices to reject, revise, or maintain connections with others speak volumes regarding her shifting priorities and values.

Jason and the Problem with Perfection

With his overly structured ways and inflexible view of the world, Jason must go. At the start, however, Jason gives Macy what she believes she needs. In light of her loss, Jason provides a surety, a certainty that counteracts her own prevailing sense of confusion. With him, Macy feels comforted, even hopeful. Just as he explains neatly the themes in *Macbeth* during their first interaction, she believes he might be able to make sense of the senseless loss of her father. Macy knows she is settling out of fear but continues to believe that Jason is right for her. She claims to be satisfied with his lack of tenderness, his subtle and concise expression of emotion. Macy has convinced herself that this is enough, believing he should not have to prove his love. She should just know his feelings. When he chooses to put their relationship on hold, Macy is shocked but not ultimately surprised. She envisions him writing the email message, "so methodical, somewhere between condensing the notes he'd taken that day and logging on to his environmental action Listserves" (59).

With time, Macy understands that she no longer needs Jason. She admits she doesn't want him back, that their relationship is over, and that she is fine with that. She does not abandon him completely, however, and communicates with him via email after he reaches out to her due to the illness of his grandmother. Although she is willing to listen and respond, this time it is on her terms. She refuses to worry too much about hidden meanings or words not stated, instead drafting and sending her replies without overthinking. She no longer feels the need to figure out the kind of girl he wants her to be; she is simply herself. When Macy and Jason meet in person at the gala reception for the first time since the break, Jason requests that they each compose a list of what is desired in a relationship and then, at a set time, sit down and see what corresponds. Macy asks him to consider what might happen if something unexpected and not on the list emerges. Jason is incredulous, unable to conceive of surprises. Although Macy wishes to help him see what she has learned, she understands that he must come to this on his own. She has moved beyond him.

Deborah and the Conundrum of Control

Macy's relationship with her mother must change in order for it to last. Interactions between Macy and Deborah are very formal, never overly personal. When we first see them together, Deborah briefs her daughter on the restroom protocol necessary for a successful social event and calls Macy a good girl when she provides the correct response to her query about toilet etiquette. Macy and Deborah share an unhealthy secret that is never broached; Macy blames herself for father's death, while her mother holds herself responsible. Each wonders about the what ifs—What if I had jumped out of bed right after he roused me? What if I had not pushed so hard for the expansion of the business?

The two settle into a routine that minimizes any unexpectedness. Dinner is served in the dining room promptly at six, the entrée fixed by Deborah and salad or vegetable prepared by Macy. After the meal, Macy wipes the counters and packs up leftovers, while her mother rinses the dishes and loads them into the dishwasher. And so it goes each night. Dinner conversation remains neutral despite Macy's desire to share her real feelings. Even their mundane conversations are interrupted by regular calls from contractors, a fact that hurts Macy even further in that even near strangers have better access to her mother than she does. Macy fears she has missed her chance, regretting not leaping into her mother's open arms the few times she offered her daughter solace and comfort just after her father's death. Now, her mother has stopped offering, assuming all is well when Macy needs her most.

Deborah works hard to control her daughter, holding her in check to minimize the likelihood that she, like her husband, will be lost. When Delia offers Macy a job as a server, Deborah pipes up quickly, reminding Macy of her commitment to the library job. When Macy expresses her frustrations regarding her new position at the information desk, Deborah reminds her that the job provides a great experience and that this is what really matters in the eyes of college recruiters. It is no surprise, then, that Macy chooses to keep secret her break up with Jason.

When Deborah learns from Jason's mother that Macy and Jason are on a break, she becomes concerned about her daughter—not necessarily out of any genuine desire to see her daughter happy but to ensure that she remains on the right (and safe) track. She tells Macy that she spends entirely too much time with her new catering friends. Deborah fears that her daughter has changed as a result of her new friends and subsequent experiences—and she is exactly right. Macy sees just how much her own priorities contradict her mother's. While her mother wishes for her to get good grades, date a smart boy, and recover from the loss of her father, emerging "composed, together, fine just fine," Macy wants only to remain in the new place she has found, "a place where who she is, right now, is enough" (221). When Deborah meets Macy's friends for the first time, she is distant and polite but quick to condemn when they are out of earshot. These friends, with their chaotic business practices, scars, and troubled pasts, are far from flawless.

As Macy watches Delia with her new baby, she realizes just how much she and her mother have both lost and sacrificed willingly in denying their feelings. She hurries home ready to tell her mother all she has been waiting to say only to find her irate and unwilling to listen. The next morning, Deborah tells Macy she has learned of her decision to leave the library. She expresses her disappointment in her daughter and tells her the catering job and her friends are off limits. Macy will now be working for her in the model home, and her curfew stands at 8:00 P.M. Macy is unable to recall the rush of love she felt for her mother the night before. She resigns herself to her mother's wishes, falling again into the pattern she worked so hard to escape. She understands her mother's rationalization and feeds into it, saying, "I was supposed to be her other half, carrying my share of the weight. In the last few weeks, I'd tried to shed it, and doing so sent everything off kilter" (304). On the surface, mother and daughter fall back into their routine, talking about nothing, maintaining a polite distance. For Macy, however, it is different this time. While she might once have chosen this life, now the "monotony and silence, this most narrow of existences," is painful to endure (306).

The stress of pretending all is well finally becomes too much for Deborah to handle. Her attempt to lose herself in her work does not yield the desired result. She is working too hard, losing weight, and lacking sleep. When all goes awry at the gala, she falls apart. This time, however, Macy is there to support her. Although Macy is terrified at seeing her mother so weak, she knows she must face her fears and talk with her. Macy finds Deborah crying in her office and realizes how hard it is to see someone you love change so drastically before your eyes. She empathizes with her mother's desire to maintain control over her out of fear that she may not recognize Macy as she moves forward in her newly developing life. Macy reaches out to her mother and holds her close, the perfect, unthinking response.

Wes and the Treasure in Truth

Macy must learn to see her relationship with Wes for what it is and to embrace it, even though it requires risk on her behalf. Macy's initial attraction to Wes is purely physical. She finds herself strangely unnerved in his presence, and any close contact with him leaves her pleasantly shaken. Her relationship with Wes begins to grow when the two find themselves out of gas and stranded on an empty road leading to a party they are expected to attend. To pass the time, they begin a game of Truth in which the only rule is that the one gives honest responses to questions posed by the other. The game serves as a vehicle through which Macy and Wes learn about one another in a way that regular conversation would not allow. The rules also force the two to respond when a refusal would be much easier and more likely. When Wes asks Macy why she stopped running, a question that catches her off guard, she responds out of respect for the game, even though she has never spoken the words aloud to anyone else ever before. When she tells Wes about the morning she found her dad, Wes becomes a part of the story, a part of her story. She feels comfortable around Wes, as she does not need to be perfect; he already knows her secrets. Macy says she has found a good friend in Wes.

The game, and their relationship, changes when Wes passes on the question, "What's the one thing you'd do if you could do anything?" To win, Macy must simply answer the next question Wes asks, but he refuses to ask until the time is right. Macy is relieved, as she doesn't want the game to end. Yet, Macy fears the relationship will go nowhere when she sees Wes with his girlfriend, eating and chatting at a local restaurant. He tries to contact her, and she ignores him, trying to convince herself that they were only friends anyway. When he seeks her out to ask her the final question in the game of Truth, she lies, telling him she wants to resume her relationship with Jason and end what she and Wes have started before it officially begins. The risk of heartbreak seems too great. Macy soon regrets her choice, however, and admits to herself that Wes means more to her than she has acknowledged. She finds Wes and informs him of a change in the rules, claiming she must answer the question he refused to answer. In response, she kisses him and is left feeling "astounded, amazed, and most of all, alive" (370).

A Study in Contrasts among and between Women and Men

As in her other works, Dessen's women in this novel provide a community of support for the protagonist, and her men are celebrated when they possess traditionally nonmasculine traits. In this work, however, Dessen has added another layer of complexity. Certain characters who share similar roles in the novel are pitted against one another, allowing for a close examination of what makes each tick. Pairs of characters deal with life on completely varying terms, thus revealing the options we have as we make choices that shape our lives and the lives of those around us. Dessen's positive portrayal of those who thrive in the midst of uncontrollable circumstances suggests her belief that the ability to allow passion to override reason every now and then is essential for happiness.

Deborah versus Delia

After the death of her husband, Deborah throws herself into her work as a developer. To deal with her loss, she "tries to ride it out as if it hasn't happened."[7] Prior to the death of her husband, her role in the business was to supervise the finances. Feeling pressured to maintain the success of the company now that she is the sole owner, she learns to be an effective seller who, on a whim, can put on her best smile. After opening her house to several potential homebuyers—providing them a catered affair and not closing the door on the last visitor until 9:30 P.M.—she slips off her shoes and heads into her office to prepare materials for those who seemed interested. Her work never ends. Macy cannot remember the last time she heard her mother laugh a belly laugh or saw her really smile.

It is not until her world is thrown into chaos that Macy's mother is forced to accept the fact that she cannot assert control over all in the world. Just before the day of the gala reception in honor of the opening of her new townhouses, the caterer quits, the landscapers rip out huge clumps of grass and a few bushes, half of the invitations that went out come back due to a postal error, the string quartet cancels, and the storm of all storms is on the way. With her characteristic obsessiveness, Deborah frets, "This is not what's supposed to happen" (345), "It's like we're cursed or something" (347), "How are you supposed to plan for a day like this?" (347). She loses it amid the craziness of the event. She is out of control; something must give. When she accidentally breaks a soap dish, she reaches her wit's end and gives up on her attempt to keep everything in check. By relinquishing control, she is liberated.

Delia, the lead caterer, serves as a foil to Deborah. With her pregnant belly and black curly hair piled on top of her head, she accepts chaos as a part of her daily existence. When her workers spill drinks on partygoers, crab cakes are eaten faster than she can make them, her toddler has a meltdown in the midst of a job, and meatballs crash to the ground, she takes it all in stride. She admits that, in her business, all the time seems to be a bad time but that she chose her profession and should thus not complain. Delia believes that sometimes things are just meant to be the way they are—broken, imperfect, chaotic. The gaping pothole that regularly stalls cars in front of her house represents the "universe's way of providing contrast . . . There have to be a few holes in the road. It's how life *is*" (93). We must live amid some chaos in order to appreciate those rare times when all falls into place. Delia thrives in the chaos, taking the disaster of Deborah's gala reception, for example, and turning it into a successful affair. Ironically, her laissez faire approach yields the result desired by Deborah, who tries to achieve the same through more organized methods.

Amanda and Bethany versus Kristy

Bethany wears slim, wire-rimmed glasses, Amanda wears her long hair in a neat braid that perpetually hangs down her back, and both girls wear sour expressions that match their petty personalities. In Macy's eyes, these girls have not only reached the perfection she seeks but make it look effortless. With handwriting as precise as that achieved by a typewriter, wrinkle-free clothes, and language that models the use of proper English, these girls have arrived. They refuse to allow Macy the opportunity to answer any questions posed by patrons, assuming instead a haughty, know-it-all demeanor that serves to belittle Macy into thinking she is unfit for the position. They block her way with their chairs and give her the evil eye for arriving just five rather than ten minutes early. Yet, these girls are not all that Macy, with her eyes turned toward perfection, perceives them to be. They may be attractive, smart, and possessing good fashion sense, but they are far from happy. When Macy looks carefully at Bethany and Amanda, she sees them for what they are—miserable and uptight. Dessen likens Bethany and Amanda to the wicked stepsisters. Although she worries that her treatment of their characters might be too heavy-handed, she still likes it, as do we.

With her blonde ringlets, exotic and enticing attire, bold make-up, and flirtatious personality, Kristy embodies all that Amanda and Bethany do not. As Macy watches her, she sees something in Kristy that refuses to allow her to look away, "something so electric, alive, that I recognized it instantly, if only because it was so lacking in myself"

(66). She wears rings on every finger, smells like watermelon gum, wears a smile that brightens all around her, and has two large scars running along her face. When Kristy was twelve, she was in a car accident. Her mother, who was drunk and driving, went off the road and hit a fence, then a tree. Kristy claims that she dresses in crazy get-ups because people are already staring. Why not give them something to look at, she asks? She loves her hair, as she was bald for a time due to a series of surgeries after the accident, and, as a result, never complains about a bad hair day. For Kristy, life is about contradictions, opposites, embodied most clearly in her perception of forever. She tells Macy that when she was in the hospital after the accident, life was very short. But now that she has recovered, it seems so long that she has to "squint to see even the edges of it" (136). Although she is scarred and imperfect, she is real and much happier than Amanda and Bethany who have lost themselves in pursuit of the impossible.

Jason versus Wes
Jason is the embodiment of perceived perfection. He holds the highest-ever GPA in the high school, has been student council president for two years, set into motion a recycling program implemented in schools throughout the state, and is trilingual, a vegan, dedicated to his grandmother, and a longtime pen pal to a Nigerian youth. In his work at the public library, he earned the title of "The Guy Who Knew Everything." He seems to have all the answers. Dessen finds it humorous that so many people despise Jason so much. She claims, however, that, as a control freak herself, she can understand why Jason is as he is. "He's very organized, very safe, he knows exactly what he wants to do; there are no surprises."[8]

As Jason prepares for his summer adventure to Brain Camp, we get a glimpse at his compulsive nature. He has not one but two packing lists, organized by main headings and subheadings. His essentials include a phone card, camera battery, vitamins, and surge protector. Like a good Boy Scout, Jason is ever-prepared for whatever calamity might be sent his way. In his relationships with others, he possesses little tolerance and is easily frustrated by anyone he perceives as slow or lazy. With Macy, he maintains an almost professional distance, as though the relationship is something that should be monitored and evaluated.

She is more like his employee than his girlfriend. Upon parting, Macy tells him that she will miss him much. His response? "It's only eight weeks" (6). Always in control, driven by reason alone, he then kisses her so quickly that she has no time to react. He has done his duty as a boyfriend and can now leave feeling as though every item on his list has been checked and double-checked. When he emails her from camp, he remains distanced, focusing solely on his concerns regarding her work at the library and the need for her to follow up on the confirmation of a speaker he scheduled for the Foreign Culture Club the following fall. He is not one to tolerate displays of affection, becoming annoyed at couples kissing in the hallways at school and any even slightly sappy moments in movies.

Yet, Jason is not a villain. He is neither cruel nor cold. He just doesn't get it. He is, in fact, kind to those who need him, as long as it is for the right reasons. When Macy first meets Jason, they are assigned to work together on a *Macbeth* project. Macy is lost in the language of Shakespeare, and Jason offers without hesitation to help her decipher the meaning. Yet, when Macy is frustrated by the icy coldness directed at her by her library coworkers, he ignores her concerns and encourages her to stay focused on what matters—knowing how to reference the tricounty library database quickly in the event of a system crash, for example. He reminds her later that the work environment is no place for interpersonal issues and that she must confront the girls directly. Further, when Macy tells him that she loves him, he fears that they are getting too close and that she may impede his plans for success. Moreover, he sees, yet doesn't see, Wes' art, calling it simply "yard art" and saying "regardless of the loftiness of the vision, in the end it's just junk, right?" (364). Jason is representative of pragmatism, reasonable and literal to a fault.

In contrast, Wes embodies hope. To him, "nothing is ever finished, or broken. It's just waiting to be incarnated, to begin as something new, again."[9] When Jason approaches, Macy feels reassured. With Wes, she feels off balance. While Jason tutors the "delinquents" at reform school, Wes was one himself. Whereas physical contact with Jason feels perfunctory and risky, with Wes, it feels exciting and natural. While Jason has an answer for everything, Wes doesn't waste words.

Wes is strikingly handsome in a "doesn't-even-know-it kind of way" (90). Upon seeing his "sculpted cheekbones and angular features" (23), girls regularly "*sa-woon*" (131) over him. But he doesn't let it get to his ego. In fact, he finds it disconcerting, claiming they can't really know him based upon his physical appearance. When asked what he looks for in a female, he argues that a pretty girl is not necessarily a decent girl, telling Macy, "I like flaws, I think they make things interesting" (192).

Delia says that Wes thinks he can fix anything, which is perhaps why he takes such an interest in caring for his younger brother, Bert, after their mother has died. When he is locked away at reform school and Bert is left to deal with the initial illness of their mother, Wes' guilt overwhelms him. He makes a promise to himself then and there: whatever else happens, to Bert or anyone else close to him, he will be there. Wes feels responsible for Bert, believing his mother is counting on him to take care of his younger brother, to help him recover from his loss and move forward knowing he has the love and support he needs.

Further, if Wes can't fix what is broken, he can at least do something creative with the broken pieces. Wes uses his art as a way of coping with his mother's death. He is a gifted sculptor. He has been taking college level art classes for the past two years as a result of an art professor's recommendation, has had works on display at the university gallery, was the recipient of a state art award, and has been offered admission to several art schools. Yet he remains modest and quiet about his talents, shrugging off compliments and choosing not to tell Macy of his several accomplishments. His art is personal, a means through which he can figure out who he is amidst his sadness. Unlike Jason, who sees any display of emotion as a character flaw, Wes not only refuses to hide his emotions but puts them on display.

The (Not So) Secondary Characters

Dessen's secondary characters once again add depth and dimension to the story. These are the eccentrics, the visionaries, the distractions that both lend understanding to Macy's character and give us a break from her struggles. The problem that emerges with such well-developed, lovable characters lies in their potential to "crowd in and try to take over the story."[10] Yet, Dessen succeeds in keeping Macy's story central, saying, "I had Macy very close to me all the time, and I was very aware of how she was reacting to everything."[11] Macy's view of these characters is key. She values and respects what they offer as they guide and nurture her in her development.

Delia

While watching Delia at work, Macy feels overwhelmed by the madness of the job, unable to imagine being responsible for managing it. Macy is amazed by Delia's ability to bounce back from what appears to be an irreparable situation. When circumstances look dire, Delia believes that things can only improve. She gets back up and does what she can to move forward. Delia applies this same logic as she deals with her grief over her sister's death. She heals herself by not forgetting, not trying to fix it, and instead finding ways to work around it, "respecting and remembering and getting on at the same time" (97). Macy envies Delia, admitting that she, unlike Delia, has avoided the truth, believing instead that avoidance will somehow make her pain go away. For Dessen, this scene is key as it "is one of the first times that Macy has been able to see that there are other ways of grieving. You don't have to act like it didn't happen."[12] Delia gives Macy a new perspective, one she first fears, then admires, then embraces.

Kristy

Kristy is one of those supporting cast members capable of stealing the show. She is fun-loving, sensitive, honest, and wise, and she gives Macy the push she needs to venture out beyond the safety of her walled-in world. Kristy invites Macy out after every catering job, despite Macy's repeated refusals. Kristy never gives up and seems to know that, one day when she is ready, Macy will take the plunge. She is right. On the night Macy finally relents and decides to join in the fun, Kristy models the importance of keeping the entire picture in mind. To know someone, we must know his/her strengths—as well as his/her weaknesses. This sentiment is captured symbolically when Kristy dresses Macy in a collection of seemingly mismatched clothes that look fantastic when viewed together. This sets up Macy's later realization that she cannot hide her scars from those who love her. In order for them to fully know her, they must know the full her.

Kristy also knows boys and helps Macy see just how wrong Jason is for her. She asks, "You've been dating for a year and a half and you can't tell the guy you love him? And, he broke up with you because he didn't think you were focused enough on your job performance? Is he ninety years old?" (133). When Macy hears her explanation in these terms, she realizes how silly it sounds. Kristy goes on to tell Macy that she is smart, gorgeous, kind, and deserving of a guy who sees her as a prize rather than a project. When Macy denies that she is worthy, Kristy passionately denounces her claims, arguing, "You *are*. What sucks is how you can't even see it" (135). Ultimately, Kristy's passion for living helps Macy see that being afraid and being alive are two very different things.

Bert
Wes' younger brother, Bert, is shorter, stockier, and just plain goofier than his elder sibling. He is known for wearing too much cologne and driving the Bertmobile, a converted ambulance complete with a cot where the gurney once was and a broken intercom system. Bert is also fascinated by the coming of the end of the world. He attends an Armageddon Club social, an annual event where end-of-worlders from around the state gather to learn about new theories. His room is decorated with posters featuring graphic images of the world being blown to bits and such phrases as, "THE END IS NEARER THAN YOU THINK" and "MEGA TSUNAMI: ONE WAVE, TOTAL ANNIHILATION" (230). His obsession with endings is understandable due to the early death of his mother due to cancer. Bert can relate to Macy's loss. When he offers his condolences, Macy knows his sentiments are heartfelt. In addition to offering genuine sympathy, Bert helps Macy keep her own problems in perspective. As she watches one of his documentaries about the massive tsunami sure to lead to the destruction of life on earth, she realizes that forever, in its most distilled form, means the "true, guaranteed end of the world" (264). Life is short.

Monica
Monica is Macy's fellow caterer and Kristy's sister. Dubbed Monotone for her one-word, bland responses, Monica provides at least a chuckle in almost every scene in which she appears. With her single-word utterances—ummm-hmmm, dunneven, and bettaquit—she communicates clearly albeit simply. It is easy to hear her various emotions come through in the context of each word she vocalizes, a complex skill that

speaks to Dessen's mastery of characterization and voice. In a fun and ironic twist, Monica is the one to tell Macy exactly what she needs to hear when she needs to hear it. Her message matters, even though the delivery lacks sophistication. When Macy learns that Wes does indeed love her but wonders if she has missed her opportunity, Monica tells her quietly, in the first complete sentence she utters in the novel, "It's never too late" (360). She then repeats what Macy said to her on the night Monica witnesses Macy hold Wes' hand as they leave a crowded party: "It's just one of those things. You know, that just happen. You don't think or plan. You just do it" (360). Monica is a great listener who is more aware of the world than many folks, including Macy, seem to think. Her timing is key. Because she says so few words, those she vocalizes take on heightened meaning, enough to inspire Macy to go after Wes even after she believes all hope is lost.

The Humor of Humankind

Reading this novel leads to belly laughter, the kind of out loud chuckling that causes onlookers to ask what you are reading. Dessen takes the mundane and makes it profoundly funny while exploring the more foolish side of the human psyche.

One source of comedy in the novel comes in the form of packages sent from EZ Products of Waterville, Maine. Before his death, Macy's father was a sucker for any item promising to simplify his life. As a regular buyer of such products, he is sent new items to try each month with no obligation to purchase. Macy can't bear to throw away the often ridiculous inventions, as they represent a part of her father she doesn't want to abandon or forget. The EZ product line contains such fascinating contraptions as the neat wrap, an organizer for sandwich and freezer bags, foil, and waxed paper; the Jumbo Holiday Greeting Card Pack with cards for every holiday except Christmas; a toothbrush that also functions as a mouthwash dispenser; and a coffeemaker with a remote-control on-off switch that interferes with the baby monitor next door and brews spontaneously. These items serve to remind Macy of her father, give readers some insight into his character, and allow us to giggle every now and then at the human quest for simplification to which we can all relate. Dessen reports having a wonderful time coming up with the various products, finding herself so caught up in her creations that she wonders if a second career might be in the works.

Much of the humor in the novel results from events arising out of the various catering jobs. Bert and Wes play a regular game of "gotcha," in which they sneak up on one another and frighten the victim to his core. Macy's first introduction to Bert, in fact, results when he yells out from within the bushes next to Macy's garage during the job they are catering at her home. When Bert hears Wes, his supposed victim, ask what he is doing, he replies, "I'm . . . scaring *you*. Aren't I?" (23). In addition to steeling herself against any such gotcha attacks, Macy also learns about the different kinds of eaters who frequent catered events. There is the gobbler (someone who attempts to eat every item on the tray), the grabber (someone who reaches for a food item even after the server has attempted to move on), and the groper (someone who spills an item on a server and spends much too much time pawing at the server in a disguised attempt to wipe up the mess). She also learns that partygoers see the help as invisible and are willing to reveal loads of juicy gossip even when the servers are nearby. On her first job, Macy learns such various and sundry tidbits as the fact that the bride and maid of honor are not talking due to a bachelorette party incident and that the father of the groom, supposedly on the wagon, is sneaking martinis in the restroom. The various catered events provide Macy, and us, a glimpse into a world of human behavior that is often silly and always intriguing.

As a former art major in college, Macy's sister, Caroline, assumes the role of expert when assessing Wes' work. Her explanations sound valid but are not corroborated by Wes who, like us, finds the process rather funny. When Caroline first sees Wes' angels, she launches into a lecture on the dichotomy inherent in the creation of angels using discarded materials, the "juxtaposition between subject matter and materials" (151). Because angels are supposed to be perfect, building them out of discards and scraps embodies the artist's suggestion that even the most ideal creatures are infallible. When she views another piece made from an old Coke sign and some bottle caps, she exclaims that it represents "the inevitable commingling of commerce and religion" (152). Wes laughs and claims he had no idea what he was doing other than using the only materials he could afford at the time. Dessen gets the humor in being human.

Layering through Images and Symbols

Dessen's use of imagery and symbolism in this novel lends a complexity that gives the work added dimension and reveals her cleverness as an author. The connections inherent in the text abound in a way that is neither artificial nor contrived. They are simply well-crafted.

The Wings

The image of the wings possesses symbolic meaning in that it embodies the strength Macy possesses prior to the death of her father and must regain in order to heal. Before his passing, Macy was a member of the track team and loved to run. When she found her stride, she felt empowered, sure that if she wanted to "it was only another burst of breath, one more push, and [she] could fly" (41). After the death of her father, running changes for Macy. She quits because there is one time she would never beat—the time necessary to get to her father before it was too late. As a result, she is diverted, held to the ground. Now she runs only in her dreams. Even there, however, she cannot escape her guilt. Each dream ends with a finish line she can never reach regardless of how far and fast she has run. Macy is reminded of her former speed on the track when an old acquaintance reveals her secret in front of her new friends, saying in a drunken stupor, that Macy could run "like she had freaking wings" (126). This leads Wes to ask her why she stopped running, teasing her about her inability to fly but encouraging her to believe that it may again be possible someday.

Wes uses his art as a means to show Macy how much he wants her to regain her strength, to resume life, even if it means doing so without her father. At the gala reception held at her home, Wes displays a new angel he has designed. Similar to the others in his collection, this angel differs most significantly in her possession of wings, added so she can take flight (368). Upon seeing this modified angel and understanding the message it embodies, Macy starts to run after Wes. She finds her stride, and all falls away. She begins running again, but this time she is not so concerned about times and speed. She instead focuses on "how it felt just to be in motion" (373).

The Beach House

The beach house serves as a symbol of neglect. Purchased by Macy's father before he married, it served as both fishing-with-the-guys headquarters and family vacation spot. After his death, the house remains empty of guests. As a result, the structure, much like the contrived lives led by Macy and her mother, becomes run down and deteriorated. It is Caroline who works to refurbish the house and rebuild the lives of her loved ones. By recounting various beach house stories of the past—from trying to cook a full meal on one burner or setting Frisbees and spare keys temporarily stored in the grill on fire—Caroline forces Macy and Deborah to remember. She later brings digital photos to show the run-down state of the house and to jog their memories regarding the memories the structure still holds.

Despite the advances Caroline suggests, Deborah still wonders if it might just be easier to tear the whole thing down and start over from scratch, to destroy the past and begin with a clean slate, paralleling her own unwillingness to recognize that there is a problem with how she is (or is not) coping with her own grief. When Deborah forgoes her commitment to spend a week at the beach house upon completion of the remodel, opting instead to begin a new building phase, Caroline calls her on her delusions. She tells her mother that redoing the beach house scares her, that she thinks she is strong because she refuses to talk about her husband but that, in truth, "anyone can hide. Facing up to things, working through them, *that's* what makes you strong" (327). Caroline eventually manages to achieve her goals. In the final chapter, the remodeled house opens its doors. Macy and Deborah enter, allowing themselves to begin the process of reconstruction.

The Heart in Hand

The image of the heart in hand first appears in the novel via one of Wes' sculptures that Macy comes upon when she visits Delia. It is over six feet wide and shaped like an open hand. A smaller heart shape painted bright red rests in the palm. The image is also captured in the tattoo on Wes' arm. He tells Macy that the design was inspired by something his mother used to draw for him when he was a kid. She believed that the hand and heart are connected, that feeling and action are linked and unable to exist one without the other. The image comes full circle when Macy finds a gift her father intended to give her before he died, a sculpture of heart in hand created by Wes. She recognizes this as a sign, a message dictating what she must do. As a result of the connection between her father and Wes in the form of the symbolic image, Macy is inspired to open her heart by extending her hand, to take a risk on love even though there are no guarantees that it will last forever.

So what is the truth about forever? Well, that depends upon your perspective and place in time. For Bert, waiting twenty minutes for Kristy to get ready for a night on the town seems like forever. For Macy, imagining a summer without Wes fills her with dread as she envisions spending the long days alone. For Deborah, a week away from work is too much to spare, impossible to recover from. Dessen reminds us, "For any one of us, our forever could end in an hour, or in a hundred years from now. You can never know for sure, so you'd better make every second count" (136). Regardless of the time we have left, we must not squander even a moment by forgetting to live. Indeed, there is only one truth about forever that really matters: it is happening (374).

Notes

1. Sarah Dessen, "The Truth About Forever," *Personal Website*, at www.sarahdessen.com/forever.html (accessed 8 June 2004).

2. "An Interview with Sarah Dessen," *BWI*, at http://www.bwibooks.com/sdessen.htm (accessed 2 April 2004).

3. Dessen, "The Truth About Forever," *Personal Website*.

4. Jeff Zaleski, review of *The Truth About Forever*, by Sarah Dessen, *Publishers Weekly*, 3 May 2004, 194.

5. Ilene Cooper, review of *The Truth About Forever*, by Sarah Dessen, *Booklist*, 15 April 2004, 1437.

6. "Get to Know Sarah Dessen," *The Truth About Sarah Dessen (and Her Books)*, Viking Promotional Materials, 2004.

7. "An Interview with Sarah Dessen," *BWI*.

8. "An Interview with Sarah Dessen," *BWI*.

9. Dessen, "The Truth About Forever," *Personal Website*.

10. "An Interview with Sarah Dessen," *BWI*.

11. "An Interview with Sarah Dessen," *BWI*.

12. "An Interview with Sarah Dessen," *BWI*.

CHAPTER NINE

~

How to Deal and Where to Head from Here

The Film

Cast of Characters
Mandy Moore—Halley Martin
Trent Ford—Macon Forrester
Allison Janney—Lydia (Halley's mother)
Peter Gallagher—Len (Halley's father)
Alex Holden—Scarlett (Halley's best friend)
Mary Catherine Garrison—Ashley (Halley's older sister)
Mackenzie Astin—Lewis Warsher (Ashley's fiancé)
Connie Ray—Marion (Scarlett's mother)
Dylan Baker—Steve (Lydia's new beau)
Nina Foch—Grandma Halley (Halley's grandmother)
Crew
Clare Kilner—Director
Neena Beber—Screenplay
William Teitler and Erica Huggins—Producers

When I spoke with Sarah Dessen, the top task on her list of priorities
was to select just the right dress to wear to the premiere of the film her
books inspired, a problem we would all like to have. *How to Deal* (New

Line Cinema, 2003) is based upon the characters and plot lines from her first two novels, *That Summer* and *Someone Like You*. Although the film did not open to rave reviews and Dessen herself was not wholly pleased with the final product, the process of watching the written word become fodder for the big screen was an amazing experience for Dessen, one she would undergo again without hesitation.

The combining of the two novels into one screenplay resulted in a movie that is a hybrid in nature. The film borrows the story and central characters (Halley, Macon, and Scarlett) from *That Summer* but steals Halley's family from Haven's in *Someone Like You*. Halley, then, has Ashley from *That Summer* for a sister and Haven's mother from *That Summer* as her own. The film tells the story of seventeen-year-old Halley who believes that the quest for true love is vastly overrated. Her parents have divorced, her sister is preparing to marry a man with whom she argues incessantly, and her best friend betrays her by falling in love despite a promise to avoid such an entanglement. Halley meets Macon Forrester, a boy who shares her jaded perspective on love. With time, however, the two find in one another companionship and ultimately the love they never expected. Making a movie from a novel results inevitably in a changed story. The fact that this movie comes from the merging of two novels compounds the issue of transfer even further. The film version of the stories differs most considerably from the novels in that Halley and Macon end up together at the end of the movie, surely a result of the Hollywood need for a happy ending. There is also the addition of a pot-smoking grandmother and the elimination of thorough development of Macon's bad-boy persona.

The idea for turning the books into film began when producer William Teitler read the two novels and was struck by how fully he resonated with the "emotional intensity and honest portrayal of family life" they contain.[1] The father of two daughters, Teitler hoped to make a film that was true to the emotions and lives experienced by teenagers. He approached screenwriter Neena Beber, known for her work as a playwright and writer for MTV's *Daria*. Beber claims that the process of making something new out of something that already existed was challenging. In the process of writing the screenplay, she saw herself as a "translator" working to convey the world that Dessen created in her books. Upon reading the final product, Dessen found it odd and impressive to hear her characters saying lines not contained in the novel but perfectly appropriate to their personalities.

Despite this compliment, Dessen is certain that some loyal readers will be disappointed in the film, mourning the loss or revision of scenes they love in the novels. She felt that way, too, for a time. It was obvious upon reading the script that the movie would not be faithful to the book. Especially disappointing for Dessen was the film's treatment of Scarlett, whose role was diminished in the movie. With time and several viewings, however, Dessen made peace with the changed version of her tales, admitting that she had a choice in how she wanted to deal with the situation: "I could be really negative about it, and that wouldn't be good for anybody, or I could kind of go along for the ride."[2] She opted for the ride and enjoyed the experience as something unique rather than disappointing. Essentially, she realized that the novels will remain just as she wrote them, regardless of how they emerged in the movie. Although fans have expressed concern that they didn't imagine Halley with dark hair, for example, Dessen accepts the criticism with grace, noting, "I've never seen a movie based on a book, hated the movie, and then not liked the book anymore. It's a totally different medium. I liked this movie. I thought it was so cute. It's got a really cute boy in it. It's really sweet."

A film buff and celebrity junkie in her own right, Dessen loved being a part of the movie-making process. For five years, her first two books, *That Summer* and *Someone Like You*, were under option with a production company. A script was written, but there were no takers. That all changed, however, in February 2002 when Dessen arrived home from walking her dog to find an ecstatic phone message from her agent indicating that the film was picked up by New Line Cinema. Shooting began in Toronto in June of that year. Dessen likens the process to an out-of-body experience, saying, "While I am here in North Carolina trying to write, cleaning out my refrigerator, and going to the grocery store, there is a huge group of people in Canada hard at work bringing characters I created to the screen. That's just insane. If I thought about it too much, I think my head would explode."[3]

In the process of making book into film, Dessen was advised by her editor to take the money and run, to avoid getting too involved and investing time in a project that wouldn't allow for her active participation. Dessen was surprised, then, when she was contacted by the producer and invited to read the script and make suggestions for revision. Upon reading it, Dessen identified some items she wanted to see changed. Although not all of her ideas made the final cut, she felt honored that the producer showed a genuine interest in her opinion. He continued to keep her involved in the process, even inviting her to visit the set. Dessen admits, "I had heard that most times they just want the writer to go away. But they flew me up to Toronto. They put me in a hotel for four days and let me come to the set and hang out and ask questions, which was really nice. They were much more compassionate to me than I had been taught that they would be."

While in Toronto, Dessen found herself in a state of awe, both over the fact that the characters and places created in her mind were coming alive in front of her eyes and the fact that this was being achieved through the work of celebrities she had followed in the pages of *Entertainment Weekly*. As she arrived on the scene, she found it overwhelming. She describes her first impressions: "There, right in front of my eyes, is the bedroom of the character I created, her kitchen, all of it come to life. Then, they show me a few scenes they've already shot, one of which was right out of one of the books. I realize, watching, that I am holding my breath the entire time."[4] Dessen was impressed especially by the film's star, Mandy Moore, a woman who Dessen describes as friendly, down to earth, and committed to her craft despite her youth. When she met Moore for the first time, she came upon her sitting in a chair and flipping through a magazine. Dessen tried to appear relaxed despite the fact that the Mandy Moore she saw on MTV the night before was now right in front of her playing a character she envisioned. She recalls, "When we were introduced she said hello so nicely, very genuinely. I think I said something about being a fan. (Honestly, I don't remember.) I was just glad I didn't collapse or burst into nervous laughter, but then again it was a brief hello, which was probably to my advantage in preventing either of those things from happening."[5]

On the last day of her visit, Ashley's wedding was being filmed. Dessen was invited to appear in the scene as an extra. Although she was in costume and set to go, the filming was running late and she had an early flight to catch. Instead, Dessen sat in the back pew watching Ashely go down the aisle, thinking, "This is so insane. This whole scene was in my head. It all started in my little house in Durham, North Carolina." Although she regrets not pulling an all-nighter to be able to see her face on the big screen, she is comforted by the words of a worker on the set that reminded her that she is the creator of these characters, and that, as such, she is already in the film. Dessen admits that she regrets not being able to pick out her image in that scene but finds "comfort in knowing, deep down, that [she is] in every part of it in one way or another."[6]

Dessen did indeed find just the right dress for the premiere, by the way. She describes the night as a whirlwind that took her from having drinks with her editor, walking on the red carpet, eating free popcorn during the screening, riding a double-decker bus to the post-premiere party, taking photos with several celebrities from the film, and eating a turkey club sandwich in a diner at 12:30 in the morning, overwhelmed and living her dream.

What Is Next for Sarah Dessen?

Now that Dessen has six successful novels and a film to her credit, where does she go from here? Fortunately, the writing process is such an integral part of Dessen and her life that we can expect more good things from her in the future. When the UPS man delivered her copy of *The Truth About Forever*, she reports:

> I shrieked. And then I got all choked up. (So embarrassing, but true.) And then I rushed over to show my husband, and we looked at it, and admired the cover and the back cover and the fact that my name was embossed and I tell you, it was just the best thing ever. Writing is SO much about delayed gratification: seventeen months after writing the first words of the book, I'm holding it in my hand. It's insane. Truly! Last night I slept with it on my bedside table, so when I woke up it was the first thing I saw. And this is my SIXTH book. Like I said, it never gets old. At least it doesn't for me.[7]

Now that number six is complete, Dessen plans to take a break for a time and wait for inspiration to strike once again. She reports, "walking away from writing, rather than obsessing about what will be my next idea, works best for me. It involves a certain amount of faith—as in, oh, God, what if nothing comes?—but it's often when I'm out doing something totally mundane, like grocery shopping or walking on the treadmill, that my big inspiration will hit."[8]

Will her writing move in a new direction? Perhaps. As she completes more and more books, Dessen worries that her novels might begin to sound too much alike and that she is writing the same story over and over again. To keep her works from becoming repetitive, she wonders if she might venture into uncharted territory, namely, telling a story from the point of view of a male character. Although she is "so ingrained with the idea of how girls talk and what girls do," she may explore the male perspective eventually, assuming, of course, that she figures out the answers to questions she has been asking herself since her adolescence: "What are they thinking? What are they doing? What does it mean when he says that to me?"[9]

Can we expect that Dessen will continue to write about and for young people? Perhaps not. Even now, she writes novels for adult readers. She has six waiting in drawers at home. Every few years, she sends one to her agent, who, to this point, has encouraged her to keep doing what she is doing well. Dessen says that she is growing with her books. As she ages, she believes she will become more comfortable writing in an adult voice. She enjoys the comfort of writing in a format where people are pleased with her work but believes that, one day, it will be time to take a risk and venture on to something new. Dessen says, "It's very easy for me to write about high school. But I don't think I could do it forever. I'm growing up, and my characters will too."[10]

As she grows up, she hopes to continue writing works that challenge herself and her readers, become a good mom with kids who are creative (like her) and funny (like her husband), and discover some answers to life's questions—large and small. When asked where she sees herself twenty years from now, Dessen says, "I hope I have finally figured out some big things, like how to really be happy with myself no matter what else is going on, and little things, like how to program my VCR correctly and make a good white sauce without scorching all my pots."[11] We wish her well.

Notes

1. "Production Notes," How to Deal *Official Movie Site*, at www.howtodeal movie.com/story.html (accessed 8 June 2004).

2. "An Interview with Sarah Dessen," *BWI*, at http://www.bwibooks.com/sdessen.htm (accessed 2 April 2004).

3. Sarah Dessen, *"How to Deal,"* *Personal Website*, at www.sarahdessen.com/movie.html (accessed 5 September 2003).

4. Dessen, *"How to Deal,"* *Personal Website*.

5. Dessen, *"How to Deal,"* *Personal Website*.

6. "An Interview with Sarah Dessen," *Razorbill*, at www.razorbillzine.com/interviewsd.html (accessed 2 February 2004).

7. Sarah Dessen, "Live Journal," *Personal Website*, at www.livejournal.com/users/writergrl (accessed 11 March 2004).

8. Don Gallo, "Interview with Sarah Dessen," *authors4teens*, at www.authors4teens.com/index.asp (accessed 2 April 2004).

9. "An Interview with Sarah Dessen," *BWI*.

10. "Sarah Dessen," *Endeavors*, at research.unc.edu/endeavors/win2001/dessen.htm (accessed 4 March 2003).

11. Gallo, "Interview with Sarah Dessen," *authors4teens*.

Bibliography

Primary Sources

Novels

Dessen, Sarah. *That Summer*. New York: Orchard Books, 1996 (Puffin, 1998, 2004).

———. *Someone Like You*. New York: Viking, 1998 (Puffin, 2000, 2004).

———. *Keeping the Moon*. New York: Viking, 1999 (Puffin, 2000, 2004).

———. *Dreamland*. New York: Viking, 2000 (Puffin, 2002, 2004).

———. *Someone Like You/Keeping the Moon Flip Book*. New York: Penguin, 2002.

———. *This Lullaby*. New York: Viking, 2002 (Puffin, 2004).

———. *How to Deal*. New York: Puffin, 2003.

———. *The Truth About Forever*. New York: Viking, 2004.

Short Stories in Other Collections

Dessen, Sarah. "Umbrella." In *This Is Where We Live: 25 Contemporary North Carolina Writers*, edited by Michael McFee. Chapel Hill: University of North Carolina Press, 2000.

———. "Someone Bold." In *One Hot Second: Stories About Desire*, edited by Cathy Young. New York: Knopf, 2002.

Web Documents

Dessen, Sarah. "Biography." *Personal Website*, at www.sarahdessen.com/
bio.html (accessed 28 February 2003).

———. *"Dreamland."* *Personal Website*, at www.sarahdessen.com/dreamland
.html (accessed 4 March 2003).

———. "Frequently Asked Questions." *Personal Website*, at www.sarahdessen
.com/faq.html (accessed 28 February 2003).

———. *"How to Deal."* *Personal Website*, at www.sarahdessen.com/movie.html
(accessed 5 September 2003).

———. *"Keeping the Moon."* *Personal Website*, at www.sarahdessen.com/
keeping.html (accessed 4 March 2003).

———. "Live Journal." *Personal Website*, at www.livejournal.com/users/writergrl
(accessed 11 March 2004).

———. *"Someone Like You."* *Personal Website*, at www.sarahdessen.com/
someone.html (accessed 4 March 2003).

———. *"That Summer."* *Personal Website*, at www.sarahdessen.com/that
summer.html (accessed 4 March 2003).

———. *"This Lullaby."* *Personal Website*, at www.sarahdessen.com/thislullaby
.html (accessed 4 March 2003).

———. *"The Truth About Forever."* *Personal Website*, at www.sarahdessen.com/
forever.html (accessed 8 June 2004).

Secondary Sources

Books

Authors and Artists for Young Adults 39 (Detroit: Gale, 2001): 43–48.

Beacham's Guide to Literature for Young Adults 12, 16 (Detroit: Beacham Publishing, 2001, 2003).

Campbell, Patty. *Dreamland: A Reader's Companion.* New York: Viking, 2000.

Contemporary Authors 196 (Detroit: Gale, 2002): 71–75.

Nilsen, Alleen Pace, and Kenneth L. Donelson. *Literature for Today's Young
Adults.* 6th ed. New York: Longman, 2001.

Something About the Author 120 (Detroit: Gale, 2001): 83–86.

Articles

"Production Notes." How to Deal *Official Movie Site*, at www.howtodeal
movie.com/story.html (accessed 8 June 2004).

"Sarah Dessen." *Endeavors*, at http://research.unc.edu/endeavors/win2001/
dessen.htm (accessed 4 March 2003).

Smith, Debra Mitts. "Rising Star: Sarah Dessen." *The Bulletin of the Center for Children's Books*, at www.lis.uiuc.edu/puboff/bccb/0303focus.html (accessed 2 April 2004).

"The Truth About Sarah Dessen (and Her Books)," Viking Promotional Materials, 2004.

Interviews

Gallo, Don. "Interview with Sarah Dessen." *authors4teens*, at www.authors4teens.com/index.asp (accessed 2 April 2004).

"Get to Know Sarah Dessen." *The Truth About Sarah Dessen (and Her Books)*, Viking Promotional Materials, 2004.

Glenn, Wendy. Telephone interview with Sarah Dessen, 3 July 2003.

"An Interview with Sarah Dessen." *BWI*, at http://www.bwibooks.com/sdessen.htm (accessed 2 April 2004).

"An Interview with Sarah Dessen." *DreamGirl Magazine*, at www.dgarts.com/content/saradessen.htm (accesssed 4 March 2003).

"An Interview with Sarah Dessen." *Razorbill*, at www.razorbillzine.com/interviewsd.html (accessed 4 March 2003).

"Video Interview with Sarah Dessen." *How to Deal Special Features*, New Line Cinema, 2003.

Websites

"Sarah Dessen Deserves Stars," at www.groups.yahoo.com/group/sarahdessen deservesstars (accessed 8 June 2004).

"Young Adult Connection Presents Sarah Dessen," at www.yaconnection/dessen/index.html (accessed 8 June 2004).

Selected Book Reviews

That Summer
Hay, Ann G. *School Librarian*, Winter 1998, 215.
Kirkus Reviews, 15 September 1996.
Lantz, Fran. *Kliatt*, November 1998, 10, 12.
Lockwood, Lucinda. *School Library Journal*, October 1996, 144.
Publishers Weekly, 2 September 1996, 132.
Rochman, Hazel. *Booklist*, 15 October 1996, 422.
Vasilakis, Nancy. *The Horn Book*, November/December1996, 742.

Someone Like You
Devereaux, Elizabeth. *New York Times Book Review*, 20 September 1998, 33.
Kirkus Reviews, 1 April 1998.

Mann, Marcia. *Voice of Youth Advocates*, August 1998, 200.
Publishers Weekly, 18 May 1998, 80.
Richmond, Gail. *School Library Journal*, June 1998, 143.
Rochman, Hazel. *Booklist*, 1 June 1998, 1745.
Vasilakis, Nancy. *The Horn Book*, July/August 1998, 486.

Keeping the Moon
Bulletin of the Center for Children's Books, October 1999, 49–50.
Cart, Michael. *Kirkus Reviews*, 1 September 1999, 123.
Darling, Cindy. *School Library Journal*, September 1999, 221.
Evarts, Lynn. *Voice of Youth Advocates*, December 1999, 331.
Kirkus Reviews, 15 August 1999, 1309–10.
Publishers Weekly, 20 September 1999, 89.

Dreamland
Campbell, Patty. *Amazon.com*.
Cooper, Ilene. *Booklist*, 1 November 2000.
H., C. M. *The Horn Book*, September/October 2000.
Kirkus Reviews, 15 July 2000.
Masla, Diane. *Voice of Youth Advocates*, October 2000, 262.
Publishers Weekly, 4 September 2000, 109.
Richmond, Gail. *School Library Journal*, September 2000, 221.
Rohrlick, Paul. *Kliatt*, July 2000.

This Lullaby
Cooper, Ilene. *Booklist*, 1 April 2002.
Doyle, Miranda. *School Library Journal*, April 2002.
Kirkus Reviews, 15 April 2002.
Roback, Diane, Jennifer M. Brown, and Jason Britten. *Publishers Weekly*, 20 May 2002.
Rosser, Claire. *Kliatt*, May 2002.

The Truth About Forever
Cooper, Ilene. *Booklist*, 15 April 2004, 1437.
Kirkus Reviews, 1 April 2004, 328.
Zaleski, Jeff. *Publishers Weekly*, 3 May 2004, 194.

Index

ALA Best Book for Young Adults, 23, 44, 60, 76, 95

ALA Popular Paperback for Young Adults, 76

ALA Quick Pick for Reluctant Readers, 44, 60

Amazon.com, 76

American Sunday School Union, 44

Are You There, God? It's Me, Margaret, 2

"At Every Wedding Someone Stays Home," 23

author's craft. *See Dreamland; Keeping the Moon; That Summer; This Lullaby; The Truth About Forever*

barnesandnoble.com, 44

Beber, Neena, 133, 134

Betts, Doris, 5

Blume, Judy, 2

Booklist, 23

Borders Group, 95

Chapel Hill, NC, 2, 5, 8, 18

Coming Attractions, 19

Daily Tar Heel, 13

domestic novel, 45

Dreamland, 1, 75–93; author's craft in, 80–82, 90–92; humor in, 89–90; identity in, 75, 76–80; inspiration for, 18, 75; as a problem novel, 82–85, 92; research for, 16, 83; role of men in, 20, 86–89; role of women in, 2–3, 85–86

Eliot, T. S., 80–81

Flagg, Fannie, 19

The Flying Burrito, 5, 59

friendship, 3–4, 14. *See also Someone Like You; That Summer; This Lullaby*

gender, x, 2–3, 14, 19–20. *See also*
　Dreamland; *Keeping the Moon*;
　Someone Like You; *That Summer*;
　This Lullaby; *The Truth About*
　Forever
Gingher, Marianne, 7

How to Deal, 8, 133–37
Huggins, Erica, 133
humor, ix, x, 22. *See also Dreamland*;
　Keeping the Moon; *Someone Like*
　You; *That Summer*; *This Lullaby*;
　The Truth About Forever

identity, theme of, ix, x, 7, 20–21.
　See also Dreamland; *Keeping the*
　Moon; *Someone Like You*; *That*
　Summer; *This Lullaby*; *The Truth*
　About Forever
inspiration, 18–19. *See also*
　Dreamland; *Keeping the Moon*;
　Someone Like You; *That Summer*;
　The Truth About Forever
IRA Young Adult Choice, 60

Keeping the Moon, ix, 1, 59–74;
　author's craft in, 71–73; humor
　in, 69–71; identity in, 59, 60–62;
　inspiration for, 18, 59–60; role of
　men in, 20, 66–68; role of women
　in, 62–66; secondary characters
　in, 69–71
Kilner, Clare, 133
Kirkus Reviews, 23

Los Angeles Times Book Award, 13,
　95
"The Love Song of J. Alfred
　Prufrock," 80–81
Lowry, Lois, 2

Maryland Library Association Black-
　Eyed Susan Award, 44
Missouri Gateway Book Award, 44
Moore, Mandy, 133, 134, 136
music, 72–73, 108–9

New Line Cinema, 135
New York Library Best Book for the
　Teen Age, 23, 60, 76, 95
New York Times Book Review, 13

Pink Floyd, 3
Powell, Dannye Romine, 23
problem novel. *See Dreamland*;
　Someone Like You
Publishers Weekly, 23

relationships, 19. *See also Someone*
　Like You; *That Summer*; *The Truth*
　About Forever
research in writing, 16. *See also*
　Dreamland; *Someone Like You*

School Library Journal, 44, 60
secondary characters, role of, x, 21–22.
　See also Keeping the Moon; *Someone*
　Like You; *That Summer*; *This*
　Lullaby; *The Truth About Forever*
Smith, Lee, 6
Someone Like You, 1, 8, 13, 43–58,
　134, 135; friendship in, 43,
　47–48; humor in, 56–57; identity
　in, 52–54; inspiration for, 18, 43;
　as a problem novel, 44–47;
　relationships in, 48–52; research
　for, 16; role of men in, 55–56;
　role of women in, 2, 54;
　secondary characters in, 56–57
South Carolina Young Adult Book
　Award, 43–44

A Summer to Die, 2

teaching writing: in public schools, 4–5, 17; at a university, 7, 16–17, 19, 22

Teitler, William, 133, 134, 135–36

That Summer, 1, 6, 7, 8, 23–41, 43, 134, 135; author's craft in, 24; friendship in, 25, 34; humor in, 39–40; identity in, 24–28; inspiration for, 18; relationships in, 28–33; role of men in, 4, 25–26, 32–33, 36–38; role of women in, 2, 28–32, 36; secondary characters in, 33–35

This Lullaby, 1, 13, 95–110; author's craft in, 21, 108–10; friendship in, 103–5; humor in, 106–7; identity in, 21, 99–103, 110; love in, 95, 96–103; role of men in, 20, 99–101, 105–6; role of women in, 102–5; secondary characters in, 97–99, 103–5

The Truth About Forever, 1, 111–31, 137; author's craft in, 129–31; humor in, 127–28; identity in, 112–15; inspiration for, 18; relationships in, 115–19; role of men in, 122–24; role of women in, 119–22; secondary characters in, 124–27

University of North Carolina at Chapel Hill, 2, 3, 5, 7, 13

University of North Carolina at Greensboro, 5

What to Expect When You're Expecting, 13

~

About the Author

Wendy J. Glenn is an assistant professor in the Department of Curriculum and Instruction in the Neag School of Education at the University of Connecticut. In her role as coordinator of English education, she teaches undergraduate and graduate courses in the theories and methods of teaching language, literature, and composition. In addition to her interest in young adult literature, she studies and writes about issues of censorship, curriculum design, and preservice teacher preparation.

Glenn is a coeditor of *Portrait of a Profession: Teachers and Teaching in the 21st Century* (forthcoming) and has published articles in the *ALAN Review, English Journal*, and *Peremena/Thinking Classroom*. Her authored book chapters appear in *Censored Books: Critical Viewpoints, Vol. II* (Scarecrow, 2002) and *Beyond the Boundaries: A Transdisciplinary Approach to Teaching and Learning* (2003). She currently serves on the editorial review board of the *ALAN Review*.